ENGLISH AS LINGUA FRANCA

ENGLISH AS LINGUA FRANCA

Double Talk in Global Persuasion

Karin Dovring

Westport, Connecticut
London

Library of Congress Cataloging-in-Publication Data

Dovring, Karin.
    English as lingua franca : double talk in global persuasion /
Karin Dovring.
        p.   cm.
    Includes bibliographical references (p.) and index.
    ISBN 0–275–95878–7 (alk. paper)
        1. English language—Variation—Foreign countries. 2. English
    language—Political aspects—Foreign countries. 3. English
    language—Social aspects—Foreign countries. 4. English language—
    Terms and phrases. 5. Communication, International. 6. English
    language—Semantics. 7. English language—Euphemism.
    8. Intercultural communication.   9. Persuasion (Rhetoric)
    I. Title.
    PE2751.D68   1997
    420—dc21   96–52632

British Library Cataloguing in Publication Data is available.

Library of Congress Catalog Card Number: 96–52632
ISBN: 0–275–95878–7

First published in 1997

Praeger Publishers, 88 Post Road West, Westport, CT 06881
An imprint of Greenwood Publishing Group, Inc.

Printed in the United States of America

The paper used in this book complies with the
Permanent Paper Standard issued by the National
Information Standards Organization (Z39.48–1984).

10 9 8 7 6 5 4 3 2 1

"When I use a word," Humpty Dumpty said, in rather scornful tone, "it means just what I choose it to mean—Neither more nor less."

"The question is," said Alice, "whether you *can* make words mean so many different things."

"The question is," said Humpty Dumpty, "which is to be master—that's all."

Lewis Carroll
Alice's Adventures in Wonderland

Between the laws of comparative grammar and phonetics, and principles of the practical . . . use of language, lies much uncharted territory . . . language functions such as the language of power have not been studied in detail.

Harold D. Lasswell
Language of Politics

Contents

Preface

This book draws on many sources. It draws mainly on my research and work, travels, and residences in many countries. Raised in cosmopolitan Gothenburg, Sweden's principal seaport and international trade center known for its tradition of foreign languages and double talk in its communications, I became accustomed early to double entendre in its use in social relations. My university studies resulted in a book on dissenters' politico-religious communications in eighteenth-century Sweden, whose popular culture became a threat to the Swedish authoritarian government due to their double talk in successful mass communications. The book *Songs of Zion* (*Striden kring sions sånger*, K. Dovring, 1951) prompted Harold D. Lasswell of Yale Law School, the founder of modern propaganda science, to invite me to the United States as his associate, which I was until his death. In the meantime, my husband served on the diplomatic staff of the United Nations, first in Geneva, then in Rome, and finally in Washington, D.C. Our homes in those cities, as well as my commuting between Europe and the United States gave me many opportunities to study "Bodysnatched English" in action on both the political and social scenes—an English that thrives on undercurrents of suggestive meanings in the service of political goals.

Also of consequence was my work as a foreign correspondent in Europe, my monitoring of the mass media, as well as lectures for the U.S. Army, the Peace Corps, and universities in various nations. Especially inspiring was my series of guest lectures at one of the Vatican's universities in Rome, which resulted in publication of many articles and books, among them the classic *Road of Propaganda.*

In this book about lingua franca as Bodysnatched English in our global village, I am writing for general readers as well as for my scholarly colleagues. English as Lingua Franca is for the men and women in our time who face daily the same problems in understanding double talk in political English around the world, especially when they turn on their television sets or radios or encounter any medium of communication, let alone surfing the Internet. The electronic media have made English into the universal language today—a global lingua franca. The fall of totalitarian governments have given a new voice to public and world opinion, and their countercurrents now show up everywhere in an English that has undercurrents of suggestive meanings. This has practical consequences in national and international relations and for the world's struggle toward democracy and freedom.

This study tries to make general readers and scholars alike aware of these challenges in communication that are faced by citizens of the world who may either have English as a mother tongue or use English as a lingua franca.

If this book were to have a dedication, it should be to all the men and women of many nationalities, cultures, and professions who made me realize the vast scope of my topic and my own limitations to master it.

Introduction

International English is a gift to mankind when it comes to science and technology, civil aviation, and the postal service. Everybody knows what the other fellow is talking about during travels on the Information Superhighway. But in international relations of politics and culture, information soon turns into communication by the use of various communities' social values. The Internet's English becomes a universal lingua franca in uncharted territories. It is an English that does not follow established rules, but has a semantic life of its own, with political and practical consequences. Its enigmatic obscurity makes it highly effective, especially on an unsuspecting public. This challenge has been intensified by the communication on the latest contribution to technical media—the Internet. The problem there has been extended from a challenge among diplomats and politicians to everybody's concern, the more so as we become aware of the different voices from global and domestic competing ideologies and goals.

President John F. Kennedy was one of the first who faced this problem when he negotiated with his Russian counterpart, Nikita Khrushchev in the 1960s. He suddenly encountered an English that was short on ideological jargon from time past, but was rich in familiar English words that had gotten a new undercurrent of suggestive meanings pointing to definitive political goals. It was called "Trans-English" or "Bodysnatched English." This experience was soon shared and used all over the globe by world leaders and local politicians alike: they may have English as a mother tongue or use it as a lingua franca. From high diplomacy it soon extended its influence to public opinion, world opinion, and ordinary people's speech. The power of Bodysnatched English was increased daily by the electronic media's reach around the world. No medium at home or abroad was safe from its influence. Finally, it also came to serve people's national uprisings in Europe and other places, and inspired Americans to question their own political leaders. It also expressed our time's struggle toward democracy and freedom through Mikhail Gorbachev and others.

This book analyzes this puzzling communication by Bodysnatched English and its influence peddlers. Many examples are cited from different political environments or what has been called "communication realms." Finally, it suggests how we, as citizens of our nation and the world community, should be aware of the use and misuse of Bodysnatched English in today's lingua franca. The greater the challenge grows the less we are aware of it or can choose to ignore it.

1

Bodysnatched English or the Rape of a Language

The place was Vienna, the time was the 1960s. U.S. president John F. Kennedy was trying to negotiate with his Soviet counterpart Nikita Khrushchev when Kennedy exclaimed that the Soviets didn't use English words in the same way as we do. This was Kennedy's first encounter with normal English twisted into what has been called Bodysnatched English. He and his American advisors were clearly unprepared to meet this challenge. So, lists had to be made up to interpret familiar English words used in a new or dubious way by the Russians. It was also easy to suspect that there was a system and purpose in the Russian double talk (even triple talk) and that ideology was still the master of the Soviet performance.

Nevertheless, the practical result from this misuse of English was such a shock to Americans that the secretary of state in the Kennedy administration actually lectured the press corps in Washington, D.C. Many years later it was still difficult to digest, and a U.S. senator was inspired to write an article about this experience in the *Washington Post* as something new which could have disastrous political consequences (Moynihan, 1978). It may have been Moynihan's work at the United Nations that opened his eyes to this problem and exposed him to the use of Bodysnatched English by many different political cultures. Only a

very short time ago, a well-known and usually thoughtful broad-
caster and author of books on the use of English, wrote to me
that he had never heard of Bodysnatched English. He, like so
many others, took for granted that English is English is English—everywhere.

It seems to be high time that we take a look at Bodysnatched
English, which thrives on unfamiliar ambiguity. Let us see how
it tries to influence the meanings of words and concepts or symbols manipulated by the minds behind this influence peddling.
The outcome will eventually show up in the public's attitudes
and opinions, many times as a surprise to election results pollsters. Unfortunately, the public itself is not always aware of what
is happening. The most obvious use of Bodysnatched English can
be seen at international peace conferences. The peace conference
in Madrid in 1991 was a clear example of how different countries
use and interpret the same concept—peace. When the parties
tried to communicate and negotiate with each other according
to their various cultures' political and religious purposes, mis-
understandings occurred. The present ailing peace conference in
the Middle East illustrates daily the different meanings for the
same word, not to mention other trouble spots in the world in-
troducing more confusion about their concept of peace.

But there is another side to the story that contributes to people's lack of observation of the existence of Bodysnatched English. This is that English is actually the world language of
economics, technology, and sports. The same words and phrases
in those areas do mean the same thing and are understood in
the same way the world over. Air traffic control operations and
stock market quotations are two such areas. This will mislead
many people to believe that international English—used as a
lingua franca—is always unambiguous even in matters of political power, cultural life, and religious faith. But this is not so.

There is, however, nothing new about the appearance of Bodysnatched language. The phenomenon has been around for a long
time—any language can be used for the purpose of double or
triple talk (Gross, 1980). In eighteenth-century Europe for instance, both political and religious communications—closely intertwined at that epoch just as today—manipulated languages
cleverly for essential purposes. Later on, sensitive British observ-

ers of the special use of English by the British Empire's different cultures defined the manipulation as "Trans-English." George Orwell touched upon this concept in his classic book *1984*. Its definition can be put in simple terms: the appearance of undercurrents of meaning different from what the established dictionary says a word should mean. Those in electronic media discovered these undercurrents long used in communication and named them "subliminal messages." However, not everybody was convinced of their existence! Nobody doubted the existence of "body language," though, which is the most frequent expression of undercurrents in human and animal behavior.

Bodysnatched English does not seem to cause a problem when obvious colorful political lingo is used in communication, and the jargon's concepts are firmly defined and proven as to their meaning. A computer can help us to record them and their usage and then keep them in storage until their meaning is changed by an artful communicator. That change can happen any time. The propaganda of well-defined concepts such as *imperialist, capitalist, concrete solution, people's democracy, terrorist, the big Satan, fascist, communist, exploitation, warmonger, correct scientific policy,* and so on, often function as a slap in the face to the public, whether it is a mass audience or an individual. The reaction of the public's revulsion or agreement is immediate.

All words can be bodysnatched and carry an undercurrent of a new or dubious meaning that does not stem from the original sense of the word (Lisagor, 1961). A careful look at the word's context and its frequent or less frequent appearance in a message can very well reveal if the communicator is what he claims to be—fascist, communist, Moslem fundamentalist, white supremacist, Western democrat or republican—or if twists of meaning in his ideological lingo point to or are pregnant with a new direction of policy and ideas. It is here we can find the ideologue who is sliding away from his original doctrine into something new in faith or even in public relations. For instance, the undercurrents in the words used may indicate that the communist is turning to capitalist thinking, or the democrat or republican reveals not-so-Western tendencies. Or, does Mikhail Gorbachev of the now defunct Soviet Union mean the same thing in his references to socialism when he talks to the British Parliament as when he talks to socialists from Germany? What does *homeland* mean to the various parties in the Middle East?

The public is more at risk when the words the communicator uses are familiar, ordinary words from our daily conversations, especially when the topic is controversial. It is here that the chance of influencing a more or less unsuspecting public is greatest. The familiar, everyday words such as *aggression* or *peace* used in the Middle East conflict mean different things depending upon who says them. The concept may thus take on new or double meanings different from what the established dictionary states or what the computer has stored. This is a feature that is not limited to one medium of communication. During the Middle East wars it was not unusual for the same television picture to be interpreted differently according to the audience's cultural and political goals and social customs. These differences in interpretation were further enhanced by the comments of the reporters. Pictures became servants of words like all communication. The Soviet Union's mass publications sometimes used these different interpretations intentionally. The same picture of an event had different headlines depending on whether it was published in a military journal or in a magazine aimed at the public. But one does not need to go to Soviet publications to find such a practice.

There are familiar words that by their undercurrents are completely losing their original meanings, such as *gay*, in their current use. And Ronald Reagan's "tax reduction" with its easy touch on the very rich became a different concept from John Kennedy's "tax reduction" meant to be carried out across the board. Of course, the transfer of meaning first confused the public and made them hail the Reagan tax reform believing it identical to the old concept from the Kennedy administration (Mattera, 1990).

It is when a controversial issue is discussed that the double talk, new meanings, and undercurrents of familiar words arise and influence attitudes and opinions. Grammar is often conveniently ignored since it is the meaning of the concepts that evoke public response to the message. It is a communication that is often the scholarly linguists' nightmare as it more or less ignores their established rules (Winterowd, 1989). The emotional public reply is the same whether the grammar is bad or good. This is an experience had by many of the world's rulers. Lenin was only one of those who used this experience to his full advantage (K. Dovring, 1965a, 1965b, 1975). Lenin also was one who became a master of irony and sarcasm. Irony and sarcasm thrive on double talk and powerful undercurrents of meaning. The same goes for humor. Humor is, however, a rare phenomenon among dictators. It is more often found in democracies among Western politicians, such as John Kennedy. This is because humor has a deflating power that may backfire on its users, a risk no dictator in the world wants to take. It has also been said that humor is apt to reduce the serious aspect of difficult conflicts while it decreases general tension (Tegner [1870, 1874], 1922–25). This technique has not always been used by zealous reformers or struggling revolutionaries because in the insecurity of their final success they felt that their cause would be diminished when subjected to laughter and levity (Ustinov, 1991).

Common to humor, sarcasm, and irony is the fact that they all are based on our community values and alter their meanings with skillful double talk. This also explains why many people react in unexpected ways to humorous communication, depending on how strong their roots are in their community values. According to Lucien Febvre's analysis of Rabelais' jokes, the weaker your faith in your values the more you turn to sarcasm and irony; the stronger your faith the more you can let your humor play with them (Febvre, 1947).

Words and concepts may present different or the same meanings to both individuals or nations, depending on their separate political backgrounds and purposes and who the communicator claims to be. A recent example is the concept of "people's revolution" in Eastern Europe and the call for "democracy" among Chinese dissenters in Beijing. In those instances the communist concept of democracy eventually took on the Western meaning but with tragic consequences for its advocates. "Who says it?" is always a very significant question, but also significant is the fact that the influence of Bodysnatched English always risks working two ways. Usually this is called backlash, and it can play havoc with any communicator.

From the study of obvious and less obvious double talk there may eventually emerge a new discipline. Double talk, or body-snatched language, is as we said a two-way street and can be used on any controversial topic that comes up for debate. New undercurrents of meaning are not only a powerful weapon among the users of humor or sarcasm or irony. But the under-currents' most extreme appearance is in propaganda messages, in biased communications, and often in a very subtle form in negotiations. One cannot dismiss, as an innocent U.S. senator did, propaganda as "a pack of lies." Propaganda is more so-phisticated than that. The analysis of it will ask much from the scientist. He or she is asked to follow the propagandists and public relations persons on any topic from any culture these mes-sengers want to advocate. The propagandists are shamelessly interdisciplinary without being experts. They are able to handle the issue's communications with an expert's skill. Few scholars dare to force their way into this jungle. Harold D. Lasswell, the founder of modern propaganda science, was one of the few who was able to follow the performance of these interdisciplinary messengers. His colleagues in various academic disciplines had difficulty understanding him when his research was extended to cover the variety of propagandists' mix of topics and cultures. Even when the focus was limited to the propagandists' arrogant dealings with a scholar's own discipline, the analysis of the rape of his or her scholarship was often beyond the scholar's com-prehension (K. Dovring, 1975).

Bodysnatched English has infiltrated both political communi-cations and everyday commercials, the lifespans of both often are characteristically short. They are always ready for contro-versy and competition: Either they recommend a new commer-cial product or repeat or reject an old political offer. Their influence may be misleading or devastating or honest and truth-ful, both in their immediate effect and in their sleeper effect. The recurring examples of this are sometimes horrifying, sometimes amusing, and the public is warned to be active and observant. But since no principles or systems are given in the commercials or political rhetoric for their appearance as new examples of Body-snatched English, most people are still "babes in the woods" when it comes to recognizing double talk. Furthermore, most people have neither the time nor the training or the skill to recognize it. And more often than not they just want—as James Fenimore Cooper pointed out in the *Last of the Mohicans*—to find their own prejudice in the meaning of a communication (Pozner, 1990).

Then, in the background is the teacher of English who, armed with the wisdom of the established English of the dictionary, warns the public against the curious expressions that come out of bureaucracy, governments, political leaders, and others when they don't want to call a spade a spade. The *Quarterly Review of Doublespeak* becomes an entertaining read when recording one example after another of this special English. And any book that lists these seemingly endless examples can be sure to be a best-seller for a time. However, since the examples are closely connected with events in the current news, most of them also share the fate of short-lived interest—a quality they also share with political propaganda and commercials in general. How many still remember the slogan "Where's the beef?" which originated as a commercial and wound up as repartee in a political debate?

The observations of twisted communications are sometimes extended to languages other than English. But those who comment on the double talk sound like teachers warning against bad or ridiculous language use. No principles for how this twisted language is created are revealed to the public—except for its newsworthy political expediency.

Whether the public is aware or not of this double talk, the global reach of modern communication media has nevertheless made English today's lingua franca, and its bodysnatched version of twisted meanings are now everybody's concern since it is used both at home and abroad.

Bodysnatched English is not only used on controversial issues at the highest level of diplomacy. It also shows up in controversies as a daily event whenever English is used as lingua franca the world over. Our time is seeing its increased use, greatly helped by peoples' revolutions or dissenters' protests no matter what mother tongue is behind the speaker's English. Arabs on both sides of the many Middle East conflicts use it, terrorists use it, foreign governments use it, and so on. The whole world seems to be talking on television or radio or on the Internet in English. All this makes international English not necessarily a contribution to peace or understanding. Rather it tends to transform the world's communications into a latter day Babel's Tower when they mirror undercurrents from different cultures and subcultures. An American president is not the only one who is failing in his rhetoric in this respect. What did Bush mean when he appealed to the belligerent parties in the civil war in former Yugoslavia to bury their "parochial interest"? Was it the Serbs' parochial interest or the Croatians' or both? The undercurrents of meaning from his own American background obviously tried to cover many centuries' differences in culture and nationalism among the people. This could not easily be dismissed as only "parochial interest" in the American sense. The speaker was very much abroad both geographically and as a communicator.

The different ages of culture and the different purposes and ideas also show up not only in the war in the former Yugoslavia, but are present in other conflicts when a common lingua franca is used. Everybody may use the same identical words—parochial interest, for instance—keeping their familiar appearance on the surface. This is the common ground, but anyone who cannot see further than this is easily persuaded that we all have so much in common. But look at the interpretation of the words "democracy" or "human rights," for instance. "Human rights are just dollar imperialism to suppress the masses," declared the People's Republic of China recently. "Democracy means law and order," said the later-deposed Romanian president in the best tradition of *1984*. The vague meaning of democracy is also illustrated when the president of Iraq uses it or when the president of the United States identifies with the concept or the emir in Kuwait promises it. The different undercurrents of diversified meanings risk dividing people rather than uniting them in the long run. In the meantime, the lingua franca's seemingly familiar English links together the most different cultures through today's communication media and feigns similarity despite the differences in meanings. This surface link is so important as a first step in communication among nations that famous linguists throughout history have pointed out that language is the most important communication media, widely surpassing all kinds of modern technology in communication. Current proof of this is the fact that when television really wants to emphasize a message it lets its pictures be accompanied by letters and figures on the screen (Kozol, 1985; Tegner [1870, 1874], 1922–25). But this does not reduce the importance of the role of technology and its innovations we witness in our time. In fact, they have made language more important than ever. The promotion of English as a world language—a lingua franca—is happening on a scale never experienced before (Wright, 1990).

Worldwide modern electronic media, as well as globally threatening economic disasters, have forced today's opening up of communications—*glasnost*—by totalitarian powers to the rest of the world. This has made English as lingua franca and its bodysnatched version one of the age's dominant communication problems. This is because the public and their leaders do not always mean identical things when using identical phrases and words. The problem worsens when we soon discover that what we don't have in common, we cannot communicate.

There is hardly one aspect of human life in which English and its bodysnatched version do not appear today. Everybody uses it, and the bodysnatched version may be used purposefully or not. In a dramatic way it concerns war or peace and national security. And the more our world moves from cold war to coexistence by communication and trade wars, the more opportunities there are for Bodysnatched English to create understanding and misunderstanding. Often communication is brushed aside as "mere rhetoric" or "theater" when a politician, in or out of power, talks with his public about an opponent's performance. But political rhetoric is often intended to prepare the public for future action or nonaction. In some countries people's lives depend on the kind of rhetoric and theater that is offered.

Communication is, above all, an art. This is an aspect researchers seldom take into account. They forget that theater has always offered catharsis. All this also touches the communication of news, diplomacy, negotiations, science, entertainment, art and literature, religion, politics, trade, business, and transportation, not to mention all the cases when music and songs as well as poetry serve a special purpose. It influences in a very practical way any policy and public opinion. One meets it not only in professional diplomacy, but also in today's "public diplomacy."

This is a term not only for the communicator's so-called leveling with the public but also for the public's opinion, both at home and abroad when it communicates back to the communicator and on its own initiative talks to the power holders and brokers. Both world opinion and public opinion at home are strong participants here. On a large scale we have examples of this in Eastern Europe's "people's revolution" and among dissenters in the People's Republic of China, among the Kurds in Iraq, and in many other places.

Therefore, performance before a mass public, at home and abroad, requires artistic skill, play acting, and creativity from a successful communicator. So, he or she must be a born artist, an actor who describes reality according to his or her purpose or vision—or script—that is interpreted through the actor's personality. At the same time the communicator must take into account both his or her and the public's values. That is why Eva Peron succeeded in identifying the "nature of women"—an ambivalent concept—as "perfect Peronista." Both she and her public had a common ground in their Catholic upbringing. She relentlessly challenged the values of the Catholic faith with the undercurrents of her ideological double talk. The Virgin Mary took on more and more the face of "Evita," the ardent Peronista, who promised political salvation and social liberation for the women of Argentina if their nature became the nature of Peron. She depended on her artistic skill to lead her public's former interpretation of the nature of women into her own special Peronista concept and to a reaction fulfilling her purpose.

Sometimes, the communicator's design coincides with reality, sometimes not. Sometimes the performance is carried over into illusions and pure fiction and becomes an active servant of propaganda, as in Eva Peron's speeches. However it would be a mistake to believe that this is a feature that appears only in the speeches of a dictator. Information aimed at persuasion is easily twisted into propaganda, whoever the communicator may be or whatever his belief or goals (K. Dovring, 1959, 1975). This means that a special bias takes over the reality of the facts in a message and all facts are more or less presented in the light of the bias. That is, in the case of Eva Peron, her Peronist interpretation of the nature of women becomes a nature loyal to Peron.

The communicator's performance as an actor, the face he wants to present to the public, does not necessarily mean that the communicator parrots a script of foreign or domestic origin (even though the first professional actors in Greece were called hypocrites or even worse names). The stench of such name calling created a reputation that has followed them through the centuries (Mitford, 1953). As discussed, the communicators can sincerely believe in and identify with their role and message, but their *technique* in delivering the message must be an actor's. This they must do because their public does not respond to a message that does not mirror at least some of the audience's familiar interest, cast in the favorable or unfavorable light of their well-known values. There was a reason why Senator Murphy of California, a professional actor, always went out and took a look at his audience before talking to them. Then, you don't recommend that the farmers in the American Cornbelt have a "correct policy in their village." They wouldn't understand this jargon which was familiar talk among the farmers in communist Bulgaria. "Correct policy" was the familiar catchword for the communist government's supervision of the labor in the countryside. *Correct* is a slogan all over the communist world echoing Lenin's own vocabulary and his teaching of communism as a "correct science." In today's People's Republic of China, "incorrect political speech" is a severely punished crime, but the concept is now invading even Western democracies. Not long ago the concept of "politically correct" minds and language was recommended in some institutions of higher learning in the United States. The city of New York, for instance, wanted its schools to use politically correct textbooks. But long before this, a well-known U.S. senator returned from a peace conference with representatives from Vietnam and insisted that his American audience work for a "correct solution to peace." It is questionable whether the undercurrents of meaning in the use of the concept were made in the United States.

Nevertheless, as in all practical situations, even common values such as "policy" cover crosscurrents of interests that must be reconciled on the surface if the communicator wants to reach as large an audience as possible. For instance, communist rulers have great difficulty, lately, communicating socialist doctrines or collectivism when free enterprise ideas—as a capitalist under-current—pave their way into their talk as a solution to economic problems. Gorbachev wanted it both ways. He emphasized that he was a good Leninist despite his capitalist undercurrent when he used the concept of socialism. It is in these cases, among others, that the communicator's ability to act faces its greatest challenge. He may want to stay faithful to the old doctrine or dispose of it. Hardliners' talk, with its stiff compliance to orthodox ideas and vocabularies, don't work today on either a domestic or a global public. Therefore, imprisoned hostages are called "guests" by their Middle East jailers.

It is well known that power over communication equals power. Witness the eager takeover of broadcasting and television stations by any political coup. But that is not enough. If the communicators themselves are wanting in skill and art, their increasingly influential understudies in public relations usually do the job for them without being responsible for the social and political consequences of their substitute performance. "Handling" is the latest term for this, and it is more than ghostwriting.

The effect on the public has been studied by various kinds of social scientists and in opinion polls. Gallup and his associates had early predecessors and are only the latest in a long tradition of opinion takers.

The first time an opinion poll was taken was probably when the Nordic god, Balder, was slain and the other gods wanted to call him back from the land of the dead. They carried out a global opinion poll across the world, asking all gods, people, animals, trees, and rocks for their opinion on the issue. Unfortunately, evil spirits prevented the success by voting *no*. Snorre Sturluson, who lived from A.D. 1179–1241, reports this in his classic, *Icelandic Edda*. But even at this early date it was long after the event! This did not discourage the German Wissenschaft Akademie in Berlin in the eighteenth century from giving its grand prize to the multilingual and much learned professor Johann D. Michaelis of Göttingen University for his opinion survey. He presented an opinion poll on seventy-two different languages and how each of them coped with language's influence on opinions and opinions' influence on language. It was written in the artistic, elegant French of the Age of the Enlightenment but with German thoroughness, as the pleased academy announced when they published his poll (Tegner [1874], 1922–25).

However, the strong interest in opinion polls is hardly matched by a strong attention of scholars when it comes to the observation of the communicators' own designs in communications, the core of their artful creativity. How the communicators create their messages, has more often than not been reverently ignored. One aide to the former president Ronald Reagan—"the great communicator," according to many—pointed out that neither the press, nor the public, nor his presidential staff questioned how the president created his public messages and turned hard facts into digestible fiction and words (Anderson, 1988). This lack of curiosity and interest and observation of the communicator as a creative artist is more a habit than an exception among the public opinion experts.

Let us take a look at this creativity as it is the basis of Bodysnatched English, not the least in political life. Or is it a place where even angels fear to tread?

2

A New Babel's Tower

When terrorists murder innocent hostages they often announce the crime as an *execution*. It is a legal term, internationally recognized as a means of annihilating convicts who have been declared guilty by the process of law. By this, the public at home and abroad is expected to understand that justice has been done. In fact, the term has been bodysnatched to justify a political act. Many reporters in the media then refer to the event as an execution. Their mechanical repetition of the term thus lends credibility to the terrorists' propaganda, which used an accepted legal term with an undercurrent of political purpose for their own benefit.

When the Bolsheviks (before the 1917 revolution) had to raise funds for their party, they sometimes robbed Russian banks. They called the crime *expropriation*. This is also a legal term, but in this case it was misused to justify a political program. Political hostages called *guests* are also an example of the same Bodysnatched English.

When John F. Kennedy was president of the United States, he negotiated with the Soviet chairman, Nikita Khrushchev, in Vienna in the 1960s and met the same phenomenon. It was soon observed that the Russians—on purpose—used English words in another way than the Americans would use them. Lists had to be made to interpret the strange use of familiar words. France's General de Gaulle had a similar experience when in Moscow he was faced with a political French which was certainly not approved by the *Académie Française* (Sokolov, 1985). Eva Peron was a master in bodysnatched Spanish when she reached out to fellow fascists both in Argentina and to Spanish-speaking people beyond her nation's borders. The once divided Germany had daily exposure to a use of the German language where its meanings were made in Moscow (Übersetzer-deutsch der Sovietzonalen Machthaber) (K. Dovring, 1965a, 1965b). It is a shorthand German where even the grammar was inspired by the Soviet hardline communists and their political outlook on life.

The leaders of the People's Republic of China were not to be left behind in this reshaping of old established languages for political aims. Their students of English, for instance, were ordered to "speak Chinese in foreign languages" from early on (K. Dovring, 1987). That is, they should try to use familiar English words but give their meaning an ideological twist favorable to Chinese communist ideas so they could influence an internationally unaware public into the communist way of thinking. But it is in the nature of Bodysnatched English that the process can work both ways as was amply illustrated by the dissenters in Tiananmen Square in Beijing (Gate to Heavenly Peace). The young intellectuals' and workers' uprising under the banner of *democracy* and *equality* and under the eyes of the image of the American Statue of Liberty gave the ruling junta bloody proof of what may happen when the students were ordered to speak Chinese communism in foreign languages. The process backfired and foreign ideas and values took over under the cover of linguistics.

Hardliners among the Soviets warned their fellow countrymen early on to look out for the influence of "capitalist, imperialist" concepts that might creep into their outlook on life when they were exposed to the bodysnatched language in foreign conversations, especially on economic matters (K. Dovring, 1965a). And to the authoritarian mind, the worst fear was confirmed when Eastern European countries started to head successfully toward

Western values in their communication of political goals, often after expressing them to the rest of the world in English.

It seems that Alice in Wonderland's Humpty Dumpty expressed a common law for political communications in any language when he explained that the words he used had the meanings that he decided they should have. When Alice doubted that someone could make words mean so many different things, she was brushed aside by Humpty Dumpty's arrogant dictate that the problem was "which is to be master—that's all." The old truth was confirmed that a word and its meaning are crucial tools in communication, not only for the communicators, of course, when they try to reach their roving targets, the public, but it is also a weapon in the competition between communicators when they negotiate among themselves or when they try to contact their various audiences. Khrushchev was not the only speaker who could say that "my tongue is my secret weapon." Communication is in fact the last stand for a dictator, one that he does not give up until forced to do so. The furious fighting over the power of broadcast stations in times of uprising is one sign of this.

It is obvious that power over communication equals power. To brush aside public communication as "mere rhetoric" is to try to run away from a serious event. It amounts to a coverup of one of the most important issues of today: how leaders prepare public opinion and other leaders at the same time. Political communications are always preparation for action or nonaction. This is a fact that the United States and its allies found out the hard way. The takeover of Kuwait, for instance, was forecast by ten days of public propaganda, but nobody able to prevent the conquest paid attention. The same arrogance was evident in a world that paid scant interest to Hitler's *Mein Kampf* with its detailed plans for the destruction of humanity. Then there were Khrushchev's *New Party Program*, de Gaulle's speeches, Mao Tse-tung's *Thoughts* in his little red book, Qadhafi's *The Green Book*, Eva Peron's *La Razon de mi Vida*, and in the United States the new American fascists' rich jargon in their various communications (D. King, 1989), just to mention a few ignored signs of warning. They are a literary genre that, behind their dullness, suggests an often horrifying future reality (K. Dovring, 1975).

There are other problems in this public communication among leaders and their contact with public opinion. Latter day scholars refer to so-called "straight talk" among politicians, where the public is barred from intimate political meetings among the rulers, both at home and abroad. These scholars recommend fluency in foreign languages so the ruling elites know each others' culture and lingo and can get together on a more efficient basis. That makes sense, of course. These scholars also come to the conclusion that English is therefore not fit to be the sole communication medium among these negotiating leaders and diplomats. That is, English is not fit to be the dominant universal lingua franca. They forget that the public's right to be informed is involved. The lingua franca that the public at home and abroad can understand in our time is English. This lingua franca is the way public opinion and world opinion can get to know what is going on in the secret meetings among the leaders; leaks from their secret diplomacy and "frank discussions" will balance and check the actions that the public risks being exposed to without its knowledge. Lingua franca serves as protection of the public interest.

As we have said, the universal use of English has its serious drawbacks. The competition for minds introduces us to the "talk with a forked tongue" or "double talk" or even "triple talk" or overtones or undercurrents of meanings that change the familiar established language into something new (Noonan, 1990; Gross, 1980). This happens to any language, be it English or some other tongue, that is used for political purposes on matters of controversy. Speakers of Chinese and Swedish, for instance—languages that use their cadence to express different meanings through the same words—often use this linguistic habit when they use English and confuse its meanings even further. The result of all this trouble has been called "trans-English" by the British ever since their Anglo-Saxon tongues were exposed to the challenge. As a more folksy name for the same process, we have coined "Bodysnatched English." Both concepts simply mean undercover manipulation of the meanings of the established language for a certain purpose.

American supremacy in modern technology—a topic for denials, speculations, hard facts, and dreams (Wright, 1990)—and its often hotly debated dominance of the electronic media around the globe have helped to make English the lingua franca of today's world and is used both by dissenters and followers of political movements. It has also been made a passport across the world. It has taken the place of Imperial and Ecclesiastic Latin, French, Mandarin, and a few other languages—including Esperanto—that with more or less success have tried to function as a global lingua franca in times past. Even Catherine the Great, empress of all Russians and an expert speaker of several languages, tried to convince Thomas Jefferson, in an exchange of scholarly letters, that the Russian language one day would become the "standard language" of the world. She was sure of this. In 1791 she even sponsored the publication of the world's first dictionary on the "comparative vocabularies of the whole world." Frederick the Great of Prussia, also multilingual, was no less sure of his vision of the future. He arranged an essay competition where the winners, a Frenchman and a German, solemnly agreed with the king that French was the universal language of their time and was likely to remain so.

After studies of many of the Indo-European languages, one of Sweden's most outstanding linguists, Esaias Tegner Jr., drew the conclusion in his 1874 book *Language and Nationality (Språk och Nationalitet)*: "We shall never get a universal language in the sense that everybody speaks in the same way." (Cf. also Baron, 1990 and de Tocqueville [1835], 1945.) The only global language he could see emerging was the special vocabularies that were spoken in different countries by those whose common professional interest made them able to exchange their thoughts without the help of an interpreter, a forecast that was confirmed in our time by the world language of economics and technology we mentioned earlier. Of course, today's ideological vocabularies were unknown to him. But nevertheless he pointed out, as we saw, the principles for a universal lingo. Among his examples were the specialized languages of common interests, such as the lingo of engineers, religious cults (the Mormons' lingo should qualify today), or political doctrines that use jargons firmly defined to their meaning across the globe, which have clearly illustrated these principles. It escaped Tegner's attention, however, that he had examples of this universal "interest lingo" in his own backyard. Sweden and Germany in the eighteenth century had a popular culture of religious-political dissenters in common who sported an underground communication of identical vocabularies despite the two nations' different mother tongues. The use of this special jargon was unfortunately illegal in the authoritarian political climate of that time, but nevertheless it was implanted into ordinary German and Swedish. This created undercurrents of meanings in familiar speech that generated propaganda of political opposition, which undermined the ruling governments (K. Dovring, 1951).

It is interesting that so early on Tegner mentioned that English is the only language where one can see a global language emerge. He describes it as a carrier of rich material and spiritual culture. It is spread all over the world and known everywhere. Furthermore, he continues his praise, in its very simple structure it has such qualities that make it easier for English than for any other language to take upon itself the role of the conqueror of the world. Of course, this was in 1874 and it is the British imperial English he is writing about. American English was still the underdog before American technology in film, broadcasting, and television had shown its power in the service of universal communications. It should be added here, which has been pointed out many times, that the most important communication medium is still the language, not the engineering or transportation or other forms of modern technology (Tegner [1874], 1922–25). It is the use of language that prevents or promotes understanding among people, not the electronic media per se, which only open the way for it.

Our time's electronic communication media have been hailed with enthusiasm as a means of uniting the many different minds and cultures around the world. In reality, they have only succeeded in linking them together, creating more troubles and confrontations than unity, according to the opinion of many. This is confirmed by numerous events. The debates and communications in the United Nations Assembly in New York and in their different offices around the world are striking examples of this. It was also more than illustrated in a global town meeting in the

1960s, by satellites that tried to deliver a civilized debate between the former president of the United States, Dwight David Eisenhower, and a group of citizens in Denver on one side, and on the other side of the Atlantic, a group of students in London headed by Anthony Eden. The shouting match over the conflict of the Suez Canal used English at cross-purposes and had disastrous results. It did not contribute much to global understanding or peace. The global town meeting's time was over, or so it seemed. It was after the new revolution in the Soviet Union that the global town meetings were revived again when Mikhail Gorbachev and Boris Yeltsin used satellites for their conversations with various parts of the Soviet Union and the United States.

The global village is more than ever a turbulent place. Unity is prevented by our differences in political and religious cultures and by our national and economic conditions and goals. This is not a recent problem. John Locke pointed out in his "Essay Concerning Human Understanding" (Locke, [1690], 1979) that separation among human beings stems from the fact that one means different things while using the same words. Pope John XXIII, the diplomat sensitive to semantics, agreed several centuries later. De Tocqueville ([1835] 1945) finds this difference in meaning a feature typical for democracies where "people are apt to entertain unsettled ideas, and they require loose expressions to convey them." A latter day scholar points out that the most efficient agent of change occurs when new meanings are brought into words that already exist (Baron, 1990). We had a recent example of this when East German citizens left their homeland on their own initiative at the beginning of the 1989 revolution and created a huge exodus. At once the humiliated East German communist government rushed to tell the world that the dissenters were *expelled* from the communist paradise. They did not *leave* as they claimed.

We have increasingly learned that our societies are not of the same age or on the same level of development of civilization. We are not contemporary. Recent examples are Iran and Iraq and their associates when they have to face world opinion and defend their jailing of hostages. It is not looked upon as good diplomacy or as very wise to mention these differences in developments when it comes to nations. But it is obvious in all human relations and is often expressed without such inhibition when it comes to characterizing individuals and the unequal developments of their mind. Just take a look at the events and advice for words used in *Miss Manners' Guide For the Turn-of-the-Millennium* (Martin, 1989).

Nevertheless, despite all differences in cultures and goals, English has made its impact in all communications around the world today through modern technology and not only in personal contacts in the United Nations assemblies and offices across the globe. In one study by Robert MacNeil and others, the well-known fact is pointed out that English is the most influential language the world has ever known. He backs up his opinion with facts from everyday life. English, he says, is the universal language of air control, for instance. Half of the world's telephone service uses English. English dominates the air waves of radio and television. Movies, computer programs, commodities surveys, and postal services use it around the world. We find it in thousands of newspapers, in shipping and world trade, in business and information, in the language of the sea, in technology and engineering. And we can add to this analysis that we also find English on the Internet, in the international terrorists' stilted use of it, and in the shorthand English on the posters of dissenters and followers in the revolutionary uprisings around the world today.

The influence of English does not stop with the domination of so many various professional or social activities or public political performances. English has been described as a "language without frontiers," and it is. The study by MacNeil and others discusses English in India where, despite its hard competition with Hindi, it is rated as the third greatest English-speaking area in the world (McCrum, Cowan, and MacNeil, 1986).

This competition sometimes gets strange illustrations. Yule and Burnell (1886) present extreme examples of trans-English which have been implanted into Hindi. And anyone who has seen Indian films can readily observe English expressions smattered generously among the native speech. In light of this impact, it is no wonder that all in India who can afford it send their children to English-speaking schools so they can get good jobs later. English-speaking women are reported to be very desirable candidates for marriage. India also teaches English to various peoples from different nations. Hanoi is reported to be among the eager disciples, to quote the MacNeil study again. Then, the People's Republic of China teaches 250 million of its inhabitants the English language. Of its 1 million Mandarins, many speak English. English is also used all over the Pacific, in Singapore, as well as in the Philippines and Taiwan, in Australia, and in New Zealand. In Japan, the newspapers use thousands of English words, in addition to the legends in English on jeans and shirts and on posters and placards in bars and other commercial establishments.

If we go to Africa, we shall find English as one of the two official languages in South Africa. But it functions also as a link-language among tribes with many different native tongues. Standard English is taught in African and Arabic schools and "Creole English" is used among the workers (Nydell, 1987).

Obviously, there is a growing global appetite for English, and it is getting more and more attention. Multinational corporations use English, and diplomats and the European Common Market use it. English in space is already a fact. Scientific periodicals all over the world have summaries in English or publish entire issues in English. American slang has made inroads even among people where the United States is referred to as the "Great Satan." And no matter whether the debate is pro- or anti-American, English is the language of both the insults and the appreciations when the speakers try to reach world opinion by themselves or by their interpreters. Just take a look at the communications from Arab or Israeli representatives.

In Europe, English has long had a dominant use as a second or third communication medium. Not everybody likes this development. The *Académie Française* has always been up in arms against the growing influence of English on French, with consequences for both the language itself and for French culture (Sokolov, 1985).

Other countries also resist the use of English. In Scotland and Ireland, British English competes with Gaelic. In Wales, Welsh still holds on. It was during World War II that "Public School

English" first became "the English" by its use in British broad-casting around the world. Today it is challenged by its cockney version.

The Irish are more subtle in this kind of resistance. They use a formal, correct English which is heavily loaded with special meanings inspired by Irish political causes that are excellent examples of Bodysnatched English. MacNeil illustrates this in his book even though he does not comment on or understand the bodysnatched practice.

It is easy to see that we all speak variations of English according to our cultural and national backgrounds. In this lies both a strength and a weakness. English as a world language is a latter day's Babel's Tower where we work on unity (or at least understanding) but are split in the meanings of our efforts. We cannot agree because we differ in culture, nationality, age, and developments, not to mention having different religious, political, and social goals. There are examples of this in the troubled relations between employers, workers, and management in Japanese firms in the United States, for instance.

Everything that has been said about English as a lingua franca, as a universal language, purports to tell us how people should use English properly according to established rule—the teachers' approach (Lutz, 1990). Let us try to give a glimpse of what may happen to the language's meanings when the rules are neglected and it is used for certain purposes in political communications, especially when controversial issues are debated. This is, according to Lasswell and others, "uncharted territory." This specific use can touch all kinds of topics since the world is interdependent today, not the least in communications. When the communicators do more than ranting or chanting—as Castro and Peron and other dictators in power have done in their attempt at communicating—these different meanings in communications at home and abroad are most striking in the political arena. We can look to the coverage of various current issues, such as talk about economics or dangerous modern weapons, to find examples of this kind of twisted language.

No matter what language is used as a universal tool for communication, all of them have always been and are still exposed to bodysnatching when it comes to the meanings of their words and concepts. That is, all the time, their familiar words and concepts have been used for new or partly new meanings in political conversation. It may happen among national or international contacts, among leaders, as well as among their publics. Just think of the variable use of "self-determination" or "rights of individuals."

Any linguist will tell you that this continuous change is the way a language normally develops and remains a living medium. So it changes the meaning of familiar words and concepts, sometimes even dropping some and creating new ones according to the current needs of the time. Today's concept of "star wars" would not have been understood a few generations ago. And the old word *gay* has taken on a special meaning nowadays. The official dictionaries and the computers often have trouble keeping their storage up-to-date because of the continuous changes of meaning. These developments are accelerating today. Trans-English is more powerful than ever when it is used as a lingua franca between the fast-changing communications by political totalitarian systems and the nations groping for Western democratization. Look at Kuwait's use of the word *justice*; it claims Western meaning of the concept when alleged collaborators with Iraq go on trial.

Political communications are especially rapid in their renewal and disposal of words and their ambivalence in meanings. Practical instant goals of policy and the comparatively fast oblivion of even the most outstanding political figures of a period and their conversations increase the need for flexibility in the words' meaning. Panama's General Noriega's "dignity batallion" is not sure to evoke any emotions any more. This flexibility and oblivion in meanings comes especially to a fore when the changes appear in slogans that are the shorthand of communications in business and politics. "Peace in our time," is one of the few slogans whose disastrous consequences have made it a classic, hard to forget. It obviously meant different things in Chamberlain's British vocabulary and in Hitler's assurances from Berchtesgaden.

The slogan—if it is successful—sums up the meaning of the

communication process. Changes in the meanings of words and concepts are often done on purpose by speakers according to their systems of value—read: ideology—and their goals.

As we shall see from President Ronald Reagan's example later, this causes an issue's facts to be presented in light of the communicator's value system and to be implanted into the public's particular values. Therefore, the words and concepts used in this performance carry a bias in accordance with the communicator's purpose—if they are skillful. There is, however, always the risk that during the implant the communicator's own bias—if it does not coincide with the public's—gets out of balance and gets infected by the public's dissenting values unless the communicator is careful. The communicators may wind up with a purpose of their message they did not intend. It is there the public backlash appears. A political speaker running on appeals for "morality" cannot be sure about the reaction by his public, who for the most part is composed of sinners. But during the process—whether the communicator succeeds in his intentions or not—we can observe the creative artist at work. This is a fact many communication scholars and observers fail to realize. Or to quote a close observer of President Ronald Reagan as a communicator: "Nobody, not even the press corps or the public or his staff seemed to be concerned at all how Reagan created his message" (Anderson, 1988). They did not see how Reagan skillfully squeezed out the essence of difficult political issues and transferred them into a language everybody could understand. But it was this that gave him the reputation of the "great communicator." This says a lot about other communicators and the communication research in our age.

Reagan's kind of communication was not only a matter of translation. It was a work of popularization of the meanings of the facts that could not be presented to the public without the context of his own and his public's value system. So the controversial facts of aiding the Contras in Nicaragua, for instance, were always presented in slogans referring to "freedom fighters" and to the threats to democracy from the "Marxists." All these values were familiar to the American public in a positive or negative way, and Reagan's identification of himself in slogans as a freedom fighter and its synonyms gave away his bias and purpose. As usual in an open society, the American public had the freedom to choose to agree or disagree with their leader. By their response the audience tells whether the communicator was successful or not in his persuasion. The public response in this case was not uniform.

This artistic performance is, of course, eased by the character of communication itself. As Oliver Wendell Holmes once said, "A word is not a crystal, transparent and unchanged; it is the skin of a living thought that may vary greatly in color and content according to the circumstances in which it is used" (Clancy, 1974).

Often when the audience faces a new influence they do not realize it since the words used in the communication keep their familiar appearance on the surface while carrying a new message in their meaning just by the *use* by their communicator. This was, as we remember, something of a shock to President Kennedy and his political aides. In the Reagan example, freedom—a familiar positive concept in the American value system—is evoked as a reason for military action in Nicaragua. The same goal also serves the frequent observations of "Marxist threats"—a negative value in the American system. Thus military involvement becomes identified with freedom.

The influence on the public of such biased communication can give immediate results or appear after the message and slogans are long forgotten. The communicator's reliance on and hope for their "sleeper effect" is obvious not only in political conversations but also in commercials and teaching.

It has been said many times that North Americans have a special problem in understanding the particular distortion of their language that is called double talk, triple talk, or semantic infiltration of English or its ultimate expression: propaganda. But infiltration of English is not a new event on the American political scene. Samuel Adams, the pioneer in propaganda, was a master in swaying the public mind. He has been described as a highly accomplished artist in inflaming his public. This was in keen contrast to the Tories of his day who did not know how to talk to the common man. "He created stirring phrases with words that spread among the common people with greater effect than a whole volume of political reasoning" (Miller, 1936).

Not every culture took to and used this infiltration as easily as my native city, Gothenburg/Göteborg, Sweden's biggest seaport. Its past multitude of languages as it was settled by different nationalities never became a threat to the unity of the city, although it is extremely small when compared with the United States and its varied languages and cultures.

In 1624 the protocols of Gothenburg's city council were written in Swedish, German, and Dutch, a practice that continued until 1670. The city ordinance of 1624 also decreed that the city council should be made up of four Swedes, three Dutchmen, three Germans, and two Scots—an attempt to faithfully mirror the city's population and the different languages used in Gothenburg at that time. The Scottish influence and its language was much greater than the two city council members' number indicated. The city's commercial sea trade with Great Britain was already very lively, and the city eventually acquired the nickname "Little London."

This mixture of languages and nationalities not only made Gothenburg a kind of Babel's Tower, but it also influenced the population's special accent and keen ability to understand and use double talk and double entendre. Generations later it showed up as a bodysnatched Swedish when Swedish finally became the official language of the city. But even nowadays this keen awareness of double talk and double entendre makes the people of Gothenburg known for their fast wit, "forked tongue," and double talk and puns not always appreciated by the rest of Sweden. Many became confused and even angry when facing a Gothenburg conversation where the "same words meant so many different things," to quote again Alice in Wonderland.

In the United States, it sometimes seems as if many among us still have trouble living up to the skill of the early American natives. According to legend, centuries ago they met the early immigrants with the famous observation "you speak with a forked tongue." Today most words are taken at their face value by the vast majority. They become understood according to Webster's dictionary and other helpful authorities.

Why this attempt at simplemindedness and stiff adherence to the dictionary definition of words? The explanation lies in our history as an open society. The many immigrants who helped to build up the United States represented many languages, countries, cultures, races, and religious and political faiths. Everyone brought their own identity to the new land. An extreme example was the tongue-in-cheek suggestion that even the cannibals among the immigrants should have the right to exercise their native customs in their new country! But the differences in the population came to a head in a more serious manner. The Swedes in Urbana, Illinois, were chased out of town and had to settle in the nearby town of Paxton. Their accent, way of dressing, and customs were too much to digest for Urbana at the time. And Mark Twain, who wrote *Huckleberry Finn* in several dialects, acquainted us with Puddenhead Wilson from New England whose regional speech and Yankee humor was not immediately understood in Missouri.

However, to survive as a nation the country needed to create its own special identity while drawing on the resources of all its foreign cultures. There were obvious reasons for calling the country a "melting pot," or to express it in a famous formula: "E Pluribus Unum." When the different features matured into a national identity of its own, the nation was strong enough culturally to tolerate regional differences in the use of the same language. The refusal of new immigrants to learn English and stick to their native language only, was a disturbing factor. Meantime, we still hear regional accents in the United States today as a reminder of people's different roots. But no language, not even English, has yet been declared the official language of all the United States. Some see this as a national weakness, opening the door to the Spanish invasion of language and culture, for instance, and eventually resulting in the secession of some states. They fear it threatens national unity just as the use of French developed into political demands for a separate nation in Canada, where English is predominantly spoken. Some see it as an obstacle to the education of minorities and as an obstacle to their job opportunities when these new immigrants and their children demand bilingual training for an English-dominated job market. To others, the openness to different languages and cultures is a sign of political confidence and national security (Porter, 1991).

Modern electronic media, such as radio and television, have had their share of creating this attempt at national cultural maturity. In their efforts to reach a national audience—literate or illiterate—the regional variations of English are polished into a specific American profile. This attempt covers vocabulary, pronunciation, and meaning of the language. But this is a country that has no king's or queen's English as a recognized authority even in its so-called standard English. This is obvious when media, for example, report the daily news to their mixed publics. It also is evident in interviews with various public figures when the reporter's accent is often obvious. The media's short-hand coverage of the daily news in the simplest vocabulary and pictures risks making the same impact on their audience as a former age's *Biblia Pauperum* and its graphic illustrations once did on the mass population. The media may evoke the public's attention and interest, but that does not grant public understanding. Their possible influence is then the stomping ground of public opinion pollsters.

The different stages of the communication process—attention, interest, influence, and understanding (K. Dovring, 1959) in political elections, for instance—are only the most obvious examples of this. The rhetorical political question "Would you buy a used car from this man?" dug deeply into the American public's value system and simple language. It was "Political Biblia Pauperum" at its highest effectiveness.

3

Lost in the Labyrinth

Today's media efforts to build up a common American English is not without side effects. Often they are faced with a public who suffers from too much appealing to their attention—the media give us much more quantitatively than we can take in. This backfires. Then the public defends itself against the overflow of communication by showing mental fatigue, a fatigue that includes their reaction to relentless technological change.

The public's uncritical and often apathetic reliance on the familiar meaning of a word is one side of this mental fatigue. There is not much public strength or interest left for carefully scrutinizing what is communicated. This gives double talk a chance to interfere. The passive, often unaware audience becomes an easy prey for the persuasion of covered meanings that are manipulated into familiar, ordinary words. "Peace in our time" has become one of the most infamous examples of this. Brutal reality revealed to the world that *Peace* in the Nazi vocabulary meant unconditional surrender to a fascist dictator.

According to a U.S. senator who experienced English as a lingua franca and its double talk in the global setting of the United Nations, the American public's innocence of the distortion of their native language has resulted many times in a disastrous misinformation of practical events in politics, both at home and abroad (Moynihan, 1978). This was an innocence in communications that had impact on their behavior later at the polls and in voting booths. Among the senator's examples is that the invasion of Lebanon by Syrians and PLO forces was presented by the media as a Lebanese "civil war" and their military forces were called "peace keeping troops." When Somalia was bombed from Soviet-made airplanes by communist-ruled Ethiopia, it was referred to in the news as "national liberation."

Some cynics have suggested that the damage is not so great as might be believed since Americans never listen anyway— tired or not. This is a supposedly important aspect of their freedom of speech that is taken for granted. This is in sharp contrast to the Russian people and others once under totalitarian rule who for so long were deprived of freedom of speech and therefore learned to listen to everything said behind the official censorship of silence (Orlov, 1991). The pathetic underground literature, *the samizdat*, handwritten or poorly printed and often distributed in a few copies and read in secret, was undoubtedly a sign of this hunger for information. Its influence, however, seems to go beyond many books on the bestseller lists in the West. The recent political developments toward free speech in countries emerging from totalitarian rule is a sign of this underground influence which now finally appears in broad daylight.

Glasnost is hardly an overnight phenomenon. Glasnost under Tsar Alexander (1850) was a popular term, but the interpretation was wholly dependent on the tsar. Even Lenin used the term twenty-three times. And Andropov was no stranger to the concept either (Doder and Branson, 1990). The road was prepared.

Listening or not, Americans may also believe that they have a great advantage in having a mother tongue that is used by so many around the globe. This, of course, makes it easier for them to assume that standard English covers the same ideas as in their homeland. It does not seem to enter their minds that the meanings in familiar concepts sometimes get a new twist. An innocent abroad, a heavily endowed American scholar who dreamed of world peace, set out to find what he believed would be the common concept of peace in nations around the world. His philosophy was that what we have in common we can rally around. He did not know any foreign languages himself; he insisted that he trusted his knowledge of English as a born American, or as he put it: I know English. But this confidence in our global philosophical unity, supposedly confirmed by a common lingua franca like English, is seriously challenged by Ayatollah Khomeini's references to *peace*, not to mention other political cultures' interpretation of that concept. In fact, every culture has concepts that are special to it and that cannot be translated into another language. A well-known example is the German word *Weltanschauung*, which is used by the English-speaking world who has found it impossible to translate. The same is true for *Gemütlichkeit*. Consequently, concepts particular to a culture cannot always be communicated. What we don't have in common we cannot communicate. Talk to the Arab world about the Western concept of *privacy* or *constructive criticism*, and they don't understand what the words mean (Nydell, 1987). Try to translate the Swedish concept *trivsam* and you are groping in vain for words. *Fairness* and *freedom* do not exist in Japanese vocabulary, nor in thoughts or concepts. International trade talk with the Japanese was stalled because of this problem—fairness in Japan is what follows from the current power position. When there was a conference in Moscow about "how to become a Wall Street tycoon and stockbroker," concepts such as stocks, futures markets, and so on, quite familiar to the Americans, were not translatable. The concepts did not exist in Russian culture. The same was the case with many concepts in agriculture, such as real estate.

Meanwhile, regional authority in the United States is never lax in asserting its influence even in international contexts. Recently a state in the Midwest displayed its cultural prejudice by passing a law requiring foreign scholars to speak "understandable English" if they wanted to teach in its universities. Understandable to whom? There were some who at once asked why the university students were not required to be a bit versatile and learn to understand some variant of their mother tongue when spoken by foreigners. It was said that it might be good for future international contacts in business and trade, for instance, to get to know the outsiders' peculiar version and meaning of English. At the same time, the English of the Cornbelt sometimes cannot pass the tests of the concept of English on the Eastern seaboard or out West or in the South. In fact, this insecurity raises its head in several quarters. It took almost a lifetime for a world renowned American evangelist to realize that his international audiences were not American minds dressed up in foreign cultures and lifestyles. He also learned that it was neither desirable nor realistic to expect that they would become like Americans and accept their goals and choices as a way to political or religious salvation.

When this struggle for national unity was extended to a world public with dubious results, it would also limit the understanding of foreign influence on American culture and eventually impair global communications for everybody. For instance, a midwestern author on the history of popular magazines in the United States saw the history of American magazines as an all-American case with only a slim foreign contribution to its history. He credited only a few English magazines brought home by soldiers in World War I (Peterson, 1964). In the meantime he neglected or lived in happy ignorance of the many magazines in foreign languages that were read all over the United States long before domestically published magazines came on the scene. Significantly they were read for their own sake and not merely as an emotional and nostalgic link to "the old country." The author's own university library at Urbana-Champaign in Illinois has rich material from the nineteenth century on this subject. One also learns from the same source that among the readers of these magazines were often very literate people such as successful small industrialists and businessmen. Some of these magazines were eventually published in the United States while others were imported. The German influence was obvious; both the states of Ohio and Pennsylvania, for instance, were conspicuous in their linguistic double talk. The Ohio secretary of state published official reports in English and German even as recently as the late nineteenth century. In Pennsylvania the official state publications were routinely issued in German as well as in English. High German persisted there in the press and the arts until World War I. Pennsylvania German remained the language of everyday communications for many German Americans (Baron, 1990). One of the imported magazines, found in Illinois among other places, was the German *Über Land und Meer*, published in Stuttgart in the late nineteenth century. Its importance to American magazine tradition becomes obvious as a predecessor to the *National Geographic*. In Nebraska there was *Der Haus und Bauern Freund* magazine, established in the 1870s and still going strong in the 1930s. It became the predecessor to the *Prairie Farmer* and other trade magazines in the United States. The weekly *Abend Post und Milwaukee Zeitung* was published in Wisconsin. New York was not to be left out in the cold. From January 1846 to the last day in December of the same year, there existed a periodical in German, catering to German-speaking "true socialists in New York." It was called *Der Volks-Tribun* and was published and edited by Hermann Kriege, who was a close associate to Karl Marx. The periodical strongly advocated the Homestead Act, which was the foremost political question of that time in the United States. Obviously, the German-speaking public in New York was large enough to support such a publication. However, according to Lenin, Karl Marx himself is said not to have been wholly pleased with his associate's American-influenced version of the concept of socialism.

The European influence on American magazines and their history and culture will certainly yield even more sources if a thorough, unbiased study of it is carried out. For centuries Europe had a rich supply and long tradition of popular magazines in various nations. The contribution of foreign languages to the development of American lingo and its richness in meanings can be confirmed by many linguists. There is more to the magazines' history than just the contribution by a few soldiers coming home after World War I!

When communication specialists dreamed of placing a journalist in space to talk with the whole globe, no one considered that the nominee's regional accent may have made his English less "understandable" to many audiences. On the other hand, bits and pieces of English have found their way into foreign cultures and languages, but not always as welcome implants. The French fight against words such as *le drugstore* is well known. The end to Russian interference in broadcasts by the *Voice of America* or the appearance of American-style television debates in Poland are among only the latest illustrations of increasing opportunities for widening horizons that the concept of *glasnost* is giving the English language. But long before this, Russian was influenced by American English. They talk about *taksi* and *tsement* and *best sellery*. The Japanese seem to be taking over the United States' economy, but when it comes to communication, American English is the conqueror. Visitors arriving in Tokyo are greeted by posters promising *snacks*, comfortable *hotera*, a dish of *appara pai*, and so on.

This inspires authors to publish books and lists of such American words that have invaded foreign languages. These books are just as popular for a limited time—as long as their currency lasts—as the books that list examples of public double talk in official English from Washington and other power brokers. For instance, the firing of an employee is described as a "negative advancement." A savings bank that faces bankruptcy is referred to as having "substantial negative worth" (Lutz, 1990). The criticism of this comes from an educator's wish to correct the language. The approach had a striking illustration in a scholarly study of *The Language of 1984: Orwell's English and Ours* (Bolton, 1984). Anyone hoping that this is a study of Orwell's creative genius in revealing the language of *1984* and its purpose will be disappointed. Orwell disclosed in *1984* how political powers use the change of meanings in language for their own political purposes. He also showed a clear insight into the Catholic church's teachings and attitudes that paved the way for authoritarian thoughts and rules in the political arena. All this is lost in the learned zealous study of linguistic theories.

The special vocabulary soon loses its fascination and meaning with the public at home and abroad. The special words and concepts are soon replaced by others in acccrdance with the focus of the public's fleeting interest. Very few special concepts survive for a longer period of time; exceptions are, for example, "white supremacy" and "We will overcome some day." They are exceptions to the rule, and their survival depends on the character of the issue they express—special problems that are still alive in the community and are a perpetual focus of public attention.

When it comes to American concepts that invade foreign languages, these invaders are often resented as a sign of American dominance in international communications. But this invasion can also receive a more favorable reception. Often one can see or hear in news media, both in this country and overseas, how foreign statesmen try to seem familiar with the American public by using the first name of the reporter—American style—when they are interviewed by American media. Not everybody could do so with such ease as the late President Sadat of Egypt, whose native Arabic already had the custom of using first names in conversation (Nydell, 1987). But Sadat went further than this. He also imitated a bad habit of many American speakers: time and again he disturbed both his own and his audience's train of thought by interrupting his speech with the dull sounds of meaningless expressions such as "errr" or "arrr" or "urrr." Eleanor Roosevelt's voice instructor warned her against this habit, as well as against using "you know" when she tried to inform someone about something they did not know. But she seems to be one of the last American public communicators who was sensitive enough to try to correct herself.

There is another side to this semantic infiltration of a language. Contrary to what the American scholar "who knew English" but no other language believed, you don't know your mother tongue well enough if you don't know something of a foreign language, too. Even the most elementary bilingual competence throws new light on the mother tongue and its flexibility in meanings by sheer comparison. You get a new perspective of your own language and can then do the language more justice. A great speaker of many languages, the Emperor Charlemagne once said that as many languages a person can speak, thus as many different kinds of persons is he able to be (Tegner [1874], 1922–25). Many centuries later, the scholar Esaias Tegner Jr. agreed: "Knowledge of foreign languages is like travel abroad," he said. "In the knowledge of a foreign language your thoughts move into a foreign area. Much that one has taken for granted when one only knows one's mother tongue and one's thoughts did not go further than one's backyard, becomes of relative importance and one's experience is widened through the insight into other nations."

There is a practical lesson in this in our time of increasing interdependence among nations. Any university or school that trains journalists, businessmen, diplomats, or other communicators should be headed by someone who speaks at least one foreign language. Fluent knowledge of a foreign language should be a basic element in the department's program. Even though *everybody* around the world speaks English—sort of—in their dealings with American media and business, politics, and culture, the English that is spoken is a lingua franca, a Bodysnatched English to be carefully scrutinized as to its meanings when it is used by a foreign culture. This creates an extreme challenge in the popularization of issues both at home and abroad.

Then there are the concepts stemming from different cultures that, as we have said, have no counterpart in other languages. We mentioned that the English word for *privacy* is well known in Western cultures but with no counterpart that could be translated into Arabic (Nydell, 1987). In fact, all cultures can give examples of concepts and words that are deeply embedded in their own culture but are missing in other cultures, even when they have a common mother tongue, such as English. When the Scottish poet Robert Louis Stevenson traveled around the United States, he observed that "they were speaking English all around me, but I know I was in a foreign land." And then he continued: "although two nations use the same words and read the same books, intercourse is not conducted by the dictionary. The business of life is not carried on by words, but in set phrases (read concepts) each with a special and almost a slang specification" (Stevenson [1883], 1966). In short, what we don't have in common we cannot communicate. What is wholly foreign defies communication.

Obviously, those people with English as their mother tongue do not have such a great advantage in their native language as they might believe when they encounter it as lingua franca used by people to whom it is a foreign tongue. Either it is a second language for them or one of several foreign languages they use. When important *controversial* issues, political or otherwise, are topic for debate, the use of a lingua franca, such as English, should put everyone on guard. The reach of the Internet, television, radio, and other electronic media the world over—not the least in intercom conferences and meetings by global satellites—all supported by a globally spread English-speaking press, keep alive the idea that "everybody speaks English." But what kind of English? As an American university president in the Midwest marveled after a visit to India, "They certainly speak English there but I did not understand what they said." The fact is that the less command we have of our native tongue the more difficult it is for us to understand already superficial variations of our mother tongue. Sometimes it can be merely the stress on the wrong part of a word that causes confusion in its understanding by less sophisticated native speakers.

A national language used as a lingua franca across the globe is, more than other languages, exposed to all kinds of influence; the grammar, the pronunciations, and above all the meanings of words and concepts or "set phrases," to quote Stevenson, which are colored by special foreign cultures. Mistakes in grammar, pronunciation, and spelling may easily be identified. The foreign accents in speech are often obvious in revealing a speaker's homeland, but when it comes to the meaning of the familiar words, the speaker's identity cannot be taken for granted. The public often takes the easy way out; the familiar word is understood according to our own linguistic training and culture. That all political, cultural, and religious systems are also systems of communication is forgotten. These are heavily dependent on the particular society's character and history and its current and past goals that invade the meaning of the communication and its patterns (Djordjevic, 1988). Skillful communicators use these systems for their own purposes and goals, which invade the meaning of the communication and its pattern. Consequently, despite the talk from Moscow about openness, for instance, it has a hard time in substantial economic and political affairs. The community's old authoritarian structure inherited from the tsars and enforced by the Soviet communists is slow to lose the power derived from the old patterns of public communications. Another example is Sweden with the Lutheran state church's century-old authoritarian pattern of communication with the people. Its lingering influence is often mirrored in Swedish broadcasting.

The solemn, almost preaching, tone of the news or of interviews with prominent people still takes its clue from the pattern of a cleric in his pulpit, psychologically speaking. When President Eisenhower visited Sweden and arrived a few minutes before a radio appearance dressed in slacks and shirt, he was met by the Swedish prime minister and his aides in evening dress and white tie for the occasion. They had waited for half an hour before the appointed air time and seemed rather shocked by Eisenhower's easygoing greeting: "Hi, are you already here." Public performance in the Swedish media was taken as seriously as church attendance long after the state church had lost its popular appeal in the socialist state.

When various communicators and their public face the concept of *openness*—a Western concept—the international public spontaneously interprets openness according to their own linguistic and cultural background. Only reality may make them aware of the fact that a speaker from the Soviet Union, for instance, may use the lingua franca with a new twist of meaning for openness. This twisted meaning is created by his or her cultural background and special policy and with a new purpose in mind. This purpose is often to influence the more or less unaware public into a new attitude toward a controversial issue. We had one example of this in Kennedy's negotiations with Khrushchev. Soviet president Mikhail Gorbachev wanted to open up the Soviet Union to "democracy" but "democracy in a Socialist way." That is why in talks from Moscow in the early stages of openness democracy meant "more socialism." This may be clear to the Russian people, but may induce an international public to accept too early the Soviets as champions of democracy according to the Western meaning. Gorbachev had a point in his interpretation of openness. Openness in Gorbachev's Russian meant "speaking out" and "political candor," but is not identical with the Western idea of freedom of the press (Smith, 1990). The safe meanings in communication go up in smoke as soon as the global village becomes real. Only hard facts and events can clarify the meanings of what is said. The democratic victory in Nicaragua's election in February 1990 was "a victory for imperialism," according to Fidel Castro. Another example was the American businessman who expressed his dissatisfaction with his Iranian employee, so he threatened to *terminate* the employee. The Iranian, used to witnessing the many executions in his homeland, got very upset and interpreted termination immediately as a threat of murder.

The problem of interpretation of common concepts became even more obvious when the modern electronic media started to broadcast news and messages around the world. They opened up much of the world and its opinions to all kinds of communicators, their faith and doctrines, and their often conflicting purposes. This made communication among both individuals and the masses a mixture of contrasting ideas (*fusionism*, Dionne, 1991) and of crosscurrents not always realized by the communicators themselves. The challenge and temptation to influence the public at home and abroad became not only irresistible to certain communicators, but it soon became a necessity for any communicators' survival in a world of competing powers. Anyone trying to communicate with his own followers and catch outsiders at the same time had to consider how far he could go in his own jargon. This had two consequences. First, the obvious, extreme lingo of dictatorships and ideological doctrines proved to be offensive and of little use. It even backfired before a public that represented many different parts of the world of the most varied political and religious cultures and social goals. Second, the extreme parlance that revealed and tried to communicate a certain spectacular ideology such as communism or fascism therefore had to go underground as soon as a speaker really wanted or had to reach world opinion. In short, the ideologue had to become a public relations person and had to pay homage to the public's foreign ideas, while at the same time not forgetting his or her roots in the home public's doctrine. This calls for great artistic skill since community values and ideas—expressed or covered up in communication—are the light from which the hard facts in a message get the special character that make them accepted or rejected by the public. Global communication was ready for a pioneer such as Mikhail Gorbachev.

When the former ideologue transformed into "public relations man," he had to transplant the ideology and its colorful terms into everyday words familiar to the world public without losing his old roots. In anti-American Iran, the evil "imperialist-exploiter-capitalist" is labelled only the "great Satan," a nonpolitical concept familiar around the world as a term for supreme evil. And the American president had to stop calling the Soviet Union an "evil empire" before hugging it to his heart.

On the other hand, if a dictator today, such as North Korea's ruler or Cuba's Castro, sticks to his old jargon, repeatedly chanting about *imperialism* or *capitalism*—ideologically tainted symbols—when they try to contact foreign publics of all political colors, the result is not only boring to the international public, it also leads to the dictatorship's isolation from a major part of today's world community. The revolutionary of this age must appear as an able public relations executive if he is going to sway the masses outside his own circle of true believers. As an American newscaster commented in July 1988 when a new direction of communications was made by one of the Soviet satellite states: The government has a new soft vocabulary, but it is still stuck in the old communist way. That is, its old doctrine was still lurking despite its new bland language. But not for long: The new bland parlance aided by social unrest was powerful enough to help overcome the old doctrine, and became a beacon of the new day in Czechoslovakia. Freeflowing political conversation is a powerful weapon. "Let all flowers bloom" almost toppled the communist regime in the People's Republic of China, and Gorbachev was finally swept away by the tidal wave of his own communications.

On the surface, our age seems to move more and more away from the obvious ideological jargons with their conspicuous, colorful words. This is true both at home and abroad. The modern communicators have to meet on a common ground, avoiding as much as possible the striking and the spectacular, and instead use a familiar lingua franca that can establish contact with opponents or the indifferent but still keep the faithful happy. In the meantime, repeated references to actual issues of interest must be conspicuously displayed in the message. In fact, the repeated references to practical, often controversial issues seem on the surface to replace the old chanting of ideological symbols. We have examples of this in the mass communication of economic issues, as in pro or con debates on taxation, for instance. That is, mass communication becomes more and more an art in public relations, which always claim to include the general public as an equal partner in a debate or a sales pitch. The former Ku Klux Klan leader and Nazi who ran for one of the highest offices in the United States not only had a physical face lift, his face lift also included renunciation of his past by his use of a plain, nonideological lingo that concentrated on the economic problems of today that were highly familiar to the public. This device was used with great success by Adolf Hitler when he started out as his people's alleged savior. And even though the former Ku Klux Klan man was soundly defeated in his bid for office, he went home in certain socially respected but naive circles. Newspaper editorials declared that the controversial candidate had a serious message in his attention to disastrous economic problems and was therefore worth public support.

Obviously, the bland lingua franca is apt to be used by any political or religious faith and at the same time can keep the faithful by using scattered references to ideological concepts dear to the believing hardliners who expect the old faith still to be relevant. Stray references to capitalism or exploitation can therefore be used anew as in the down-to-earth lingo Gorbachev used—not to mention his talk of "democratic revolution" or "correct policy or solution" in speeches aimed at resolving economic problems in the Soviet Union and around the world. Only a close look at the contexts in which these ideological symbols appear can indicate whether those references mean only what Western dictionaries, such as Webster, want them to mean. Concepts such as "correct science" are already substantial ideological ideas at home in Lenin's speeches.

However, it is not only the electronic media that contribute to the reduced use of pure ideological words. The effect of the increasing appearance and power of world opinion also plays its part even though it sometimes seems slow in coming. World opinion, with its many different backgrounds, cultures, and perceptions, did not respond to the dull extremist communication and its specific, continuously repeated jargons, even though sinister reality was looming behind the ideological passion. Politicians and religious leaders, dabbling in politics and representing different persuasions, nations, and goals, now have to follow suit in their public performances. Always they have to count on two kinds of public: folks at home and the rest of the world, which want to become partners in this contact. Thus, our time's new communication was born: public diplomacy, or by another name, public oratory, which is often dismissed with more or less contempt. However, it is actually of tremendous importance for preparation of the public for action or nonaction on an issue.

Public diplomacy means that public leaders can no longer discuss public issues among themselves alone if they want their policy to succeed. They have to consider and converse at the same time with the mass audiences at home and abroad who have emerged as strong participants in this contact. This is not the least due to the influence of the widereaching electronic media. Public diplomacy also has two urgent, new demands that private negotiations among professional diplomats do not necessarily require for their success: You must entertain as you inform. You must repeat to your mass public time and time again the same substantial paraphrasing. This is a lesson that the once presidential candidate Michael Dukakis did not understand, to his own peril, when he limited his views on an issue to one, pure, factual piece of information in answering his critics. But this recent example (Schiefer and Gates, 1989) only emphasizes what skillful communicators have known long before the modern mass media's appearance on the public scene (K. Dovring, 1959). The most conspicuous public consequence of this is the television and radio broadcasts of news and events. Even though the news and the presentation of facts are limited and simplified by its allotted time, it nevertheless has to be presented without spectacular pointers—attractive or repulsive, according to the society's standards and value systems. This is necessary for the news to gain acceptance or rejection from the public without seeming to lecture the audience. *Earthquake* is a familiar concept that evokes immediate reaction from the public. The event needs no adornments. But the concept of "star wars" needs a lot of ideological pointers to "defense" or "enemies" or "foreign competition" to be understood. However, the simplified, time-limited presentation of the news requires the newscast to become not only an art, but it also creates our time's *Biblia Pauperum*, which picks up the attention of both literate and illiterate people. The public's deeper interest is catered to by appropriately short or lengthy commentaries and articles. This demands a more sophisticated audience with more time allotted to the discussion of the facts of a special issue. Who, then, understands what and how and why is a topic open to imagination, speculation, and opinion polls.

The need for entertainment and information at the same time is not something that has come up because of the electronic media, of course. It is dangerous for both public education and a nation's policy when entertainment is allowed to dominate the information of facts (Regan, 1988). According to one of the Reagan administration's chiefs of staff, the tendency to process the activity of the government into entertainment becomes a danger to the democratic process and even to the republic itself. Another voice from another century agrees: "Humor and entertainment tend to deflate the importance of an issue" (Tegner [1874], 1922–25).

Ronald Reagan was not only an actor who read scripts others had prepared for him, but he was also a perfectionist who polished his speeches over many hours. His training as an actor was a great asset to him in this age of television. Reagan certainly understood this himself, but others didn't (Johnson, 1991; Noonan, 1990). Reagan was deeply preoccupied not with what he said but how he said it. It dominated his political leadership, and the cue cards he used shaped his own message and thoughts. He was not the work of hired ghostwriters. He prepared for his campaign the way an actor prepares for a performance. He had strong feelings and instincts for the public's political mood and was at the same time a master entertainer. He felt the public undercurrents and picked up on them in his public messages. For instance, he repeatedly spoke about campus unrest and fueled the public's feelings about it. Associates in his inner circle looked upon him as a supreme anchorman for political news, but his disinterest in the facts themselves explain his many misspoken statements. No one can deny, though, that he was a master in creating slogans and summaries of his cabinet members' ideas so that his constituents were able to hear what they wanted to hear. Thus, the line that separated political news and entertainment was blurred, and few thought of the sleeper effect or long-term consequences on real life.

Nevertheless, most successful politicians are actors in one way or another. Daniel Webster was not the first American politician who was praised for his communication skills and acting abilities (Bartlett, 1978). The balance between fact and entertainment is a risky business that puts every communicator to the test. In eighteenth-century Europe, a literary academy that dabbled in politics summed up the process in its catch-all for mass communications: "Everyone's vote goes to those who can unite the useful with the entertaining." But the element of entertainment can go too far. It may disrupt a public's attention through entertaining commercial ads not always in step with the program's character that are interspersed in a factual program. Once upon a time, news of a statesman's funeral was interrupted several times by a commercial that cheerfully urged anyone who wanted to listen: Come alive! You are in the (soft drink) generation!

Before electronic media linked the world into a global village, the jargons and slogans in communication could afford to dominate a message, mostly in two instances: if times were critical or tense—no matter what the society's official ideology was—or if a community was ruled by a dictatorship. A dictatorship used slogans and jargon as "daily bread" since it was always in a state of tension. Western democracies, on the other hand, moved close to extreme jargons and used slogans mostly in times of war or other critical events when fast action and understanding was needed from the public (Lasswell, 1927). Of course, commercial ads use slogans all the time since they are always asking for fast action, immediate understanding, or quick sales. In some respects, they are always in a state of tension or competition, not to say crisis, when they try to sell a product or influence or dictate our choices and tastes. To avoid boredom they are extremely dependent on the skill of an artist's manipulation of the public's values since they can only exist in a free market. As we saw with Ronald Reagan, this is an already old tool in political performances. The commercial ads are also those that have been most creative in the use of undercurrents of meaning in their messages as a tool for manipulating the audience and are among the elite in using bodysnatched language (Baron, 1989).

As we said before, the general public very soon found the extremist jargon boring, but if you live in a dictatorship you have to put up with its communication. The "Soviet Man" was an example of this (Sorokin, 1985). He was said to live in a mythological state of two different worlds at the same time, the real and the ideological, both in conflict. There was a confusion between what is and what ought to be. The official concept of "socialist realism" filled his speech and thoughts with cliches that made his real life impossible to understand. The language itself was undermined by it. He started to suspect all words, and the distinction between meaningful statements and realistic utterances became blurred. He eventually became an expert in using double talk and bodysnatched language. Only a true believer may find it stimulating to listen to the jargon and its colorful expressions from the ruling doctrine and what Russian psychologists have called the "assuring inner speech among the initiated" (Vygotsky, 1962). These colorful, familiar signals are signs of recognition that the dictator uses to manipulate his people and that function as "inner speech" among the believers. Nevertheless, he does not trust his people very much. Therefore, he has to control the mass of his people with recognized symbols in his communication. In fact, no dictator knows his public very well. That is why he has to control them so tightly.

In Western type democracies, the individual's opinion is asked for—at least as a gesture. This opinion will be paid serious attention when more and more individuals express by their free choice the same opinion on an issue. We had an overwhelming example of this in the political freedom movements all over Eastern Europe. For many years after World War II, there were signs of longing for freedom by individuals in all Eastern European countries. But it was when these individuals' call for freedom was first embraced and expressed by the masses that those in power—too late—paid attention to the issue before they were swept away.

This pattern of democratic communication with the authorities has a long Western tradition, and its reach around the globe is certainly helped by the electronic media's ability to cross the most diverse political and religious frontiers (Wiesel, 1988). Nowadays national and international leaders are forced—if they want to stay in power—to include in their communication more and more of their public's special qualities and demands even though they may not be agreeable to the communicator himself. The more dispersed the public, the simpler the communicator's language must become. This is necessary to get the attention of as many different people as possible. Self-determination, for instance, is a respected value in the West and in many places around the world. But its undercurrent may often mean extreme nationalism when one analyzes the context in which the concept of self-determination is used, including its use by members of the Third World. Here one is tempted to quote James Fenimore Cooper again: "All perceived that more was meant than was uttered, and each one believed that the hidden meaning was precisely such as his own faculties enabled him to understand, or his own wishes led him to anticipate. In this happy state of things, it is not surprising that the management of Magua prevailed" (Cooper, [1826] 1960).

The medium used for this catch-all communication is the lingua franca that is the same on the surface—everybody speaks English. Everyone is familiar with the dictionary's concept of self-determination, for instance, but it is the undercurrent of its meaning, the way the word is used, that will reveal the double talk aimed at influencing the most diverse groups. One can talk about self-determination for the Baltic republics—which became the spoils of World War II for the Soviet Union—but the context in which the word is repeated time and time again gives it the undercurrent of *patriotism* and *nationalism*, with heavily positive or negative significance for the different parties in the conflict.

Let us take a look at the communicators when they are at home and abroad—that is, "at home" when they are in their own ideological territory, and "abroad" when they cross the frontiers beyond their own ideological domains and circles. Let us also see what this may do to the character of their message and to the language they use to express their purpose in artistic performance. This undoubtedly has practical importance, as it did during the cold war. Its importance has increased in our time in its struggle for coexistence and cooperation while it still is in the shadow of the past.

4

At Home or Abroad or in No Man's Land

When everybody speaks English and the dictionaries tell us what the words mean or should mean, why bother with a more close observation of what is said to us? The answer is that words and their often ambivalent meanings are extremely important. They influence us and our opinions, decisions, and attitudes. This eventually shapes our perceptions of what kind of society we are going to build, live in, and create for the future. If words and their meanings were not an important tool for the direction of our lives, we would not be so sensitive to having them exposed to careful scrutiny. Censorship over these words and their meanings is one of the most feared tools, or even weapons, in political life because censorship threatens to cut off our lifeline as social beings and individuals. This is reason enough for us to be aware of the meanings of the communications we are exposed to or we ourselves expose others to, not the least on controversial issues. This awareness is the only way our reactions to issues can be a matter of individual free choice. The problem comes most clearly to a fore in political communications, at home and abroad. No wonder that power over communication is the last thing a dictator wants to give up. If he does, his power is over. History, both ancient and recent, is filled with examples of this.

We discussed earlier that electronic communication media expose all of us to many different kinds of contacts. What our hometown politicians say suddenly gets worldwide attention. What an international politician tells us over our televisions or radios in our living rooms concerns our daily life and our community.

We can talk about a "communicator-at-home" and a "communicator-abroad." By that we usually are referring to his or her geographical whereabouts. But when it comes to psychological and political contacts in public relations at home and abroad, the case gets more complicated. It turns into a famous formula: "Who says what to whom in what channel and with what effect?" (Lasswell, 1927, 1930).

For a long time the world has been used to the special language of various dictators draped in ideological thinking and jargons. As has been obvious for some time now, their communications became boring to the world public and more and more difficult for their own people to endure unless they were true believers. The messages from the dictators were filled with colorful, spectacular words such as *kulaks, comrades, workers, socialist struggle, correct policy, socialist science, heroes of labor, capitalist exploiters* and *capitalist roaders, authority of the people, imperialists,* and so on. All of these are expressions repeatedly used by Lenin, Stalin, and their European fellow travelers, and by Mao Tse-tung and other Asian and South American *comrades* in a positive or negative sense according to their common political faith and to the communicators' purpose. The continuous repetition of ideological slang continued in an increasing frenzy. Not to be outdone, other dictators such as Hitler, Evita Peron, Qadhafi, Mussolini, Saddam Hussein, or other smaller tyrants chanted about Jewish conspiracy, white supremacy, sieg heil, or my descamisados, oligarch, Peronista, Evita, authority of the people, and so forth. All were ideological concepts of positive or negative values depending upon which side you were on. All were represented in an endless stream and tainted any facts in a message until they had lost their efficiency. Then they were replaced by other words just as tainted with ideology and policy but with the same meaning despite their new form and appearance.

All the extreme ideological symbols have one thing in common. They were conspicuous, colorful words representing a special ideology. They caught the public attention easily and were identified instantaneously by all, whether they were followers or opponents. Few persons were indifferent to calls of "Jewish conspiracy" or "down with the Pope," Lebensraum, our beloved Führer, or "nordic jurisdiction." Such symbols created the "manifest content" of a message, as early analysts called it (Berelson, 1952). It was a message that could clearly be seen by everybody. But when the analysts decoded such a message, they found that there were concepts that the researchers were looking for and recorded that did not fit into the obvious ideological categories (Lasswell, Lerner, and Pool, 1952). The analysts left those concepts as the "sump" in a coffee cup and called them "not understandable." But no skillful communicator lets any bit of his message go to waste. Later analysts who dug deeper into the communicator's performance and looked behind the obvious scene soon found that those "not understandable" concepts gave new undercurrents, character, and tendency to the obvious meanings of the communicator's speech or picture. This deeper probe offered a clue to the whole message and to the communicator's real purpose, value, interest, and ideological home (K. Dovring, 1975).

However, the obvious ideological concepts one could see on the surface of a message served as signals of easy recognition among both believers and nonbelievers in these symbols. The extreme concepts that drew people's attention also created what has been called "inner speech" among the initiated, a "communication realm" or ghetto or circle of positive recognition. But this has another side, too. To the nonbelievers or the indifferent, these extreme symbols from a certain ideology created a negative communication realm and served as signs of distress and warnings (Vygotsky, 1962; Lasswell, Leites, and Associates, 1949). For instance, the British national anthem, "God save the Queen"— already an ideological symbol able to unite or inflame a crowd— would get a quite different reception at Buckingham Palace than when played before a mixed Irish crowd in Belfast. At home in the United States we have the infamous communication realm of Mafia lingo and its abuse of English. This is a communication realm that includes all other Mafia groups abroad who use the same bodysnatched jargon. It is also an example of how a communication realm can extend across geographical boundaries, no matter what mother tongue is abused in the process, whether it be English or Italian or what have you. The identical appeals are the same. A Mafia person calls for *respect*, a frequent concept in his speech wherever he lives. Its meaning certainly seems twisted, however, to those who do not belong to the Mafia group.

By the repetition of colorful phrases and frequent appearance in communication of concepts such as *capitalist, colonial exploiter, warmonger* or *people's democracy, scientific socialism,* and so on, it was easy to see who and what the communicator represented and to distinguish his followers by their response to his vocabulary. By the same token, it was not difficult to detect the negative reaction among his opponents. There are many obvious illustrations of this in every crowd gathered at an election rally, for instance. In general, the public would not put forth a great effort to protect themselves against the extremist's message because the extreme jargon would be so obvious. Few think of the sleeper effect on one's attitude when a social situation may come up later making an issue controversial, current or of concern to one's own affairs. There are many signs of this, not the least of which is the case of a white man, looked upon by neighbors and friends as a decent, loyal citizen. Suddenly he shows a strong racist attitude if a black family moves next-door to his own home. Similarly, there is the anecdote about America "not being ready" for a black or woman president in the White House.

There is no communicator who does not hope for and count on the sleeper effect of his or her message, just as any teacher does. It is another matter if the communicator is around to see it. This has been a source of both hope and despair to communicators, depending on how much time they need for their message to be transformed into action. General de Gaulle's call for "Vive le Quebec libre" aroused both instant applause and a serious sleeper effect in Canadian political life.

If the communicator uses a colorful, specific lingo, it is easy to identify him as a communicator-at-home or as a communicator-abroad when it comes to the surface meaning of his talk, as we have already pointed out. From a practical viewpoint he shows up as an extremist in speech, ideas, and choice of words. He can use his extremist vocabulary with confidence when he is in his own communication realm, that is among people of the same mind as himself. It does not matter whether they live in the United States or in any other country. The Mafia spokesman is at home everywhere among his cronies. Observe Hitler's speeches from his intimate table talks to his rabble-rousing public performances before his Nazi followers in Germany and other nations. A Soviet or Chinese communist is a communicator-at-home in the same way when he talks to a fellow Russian, to the Chinese, or to other communists who share his ideas. He may use his mother tongue, be it Russian or Mandarin or Cantonese, or he may transplant the common ideas into a lingua franca such as English if his followers are of another nationality. But he is still at home.

Not only the press but other forms of communication, such as radio and television or the Internet, extend any communicator's reach to other peoples and nations of different political creeds. Books and pamphlets have done so in times past, but not at all on such a scale as the electronic media today. No modern communicator can take for granted that the whole world is not listening to or monitoring his performance. The global audience is no longer the Voice of America's prerogative. However, if one takes a wider view it must be noted here that in the long run books are still the most efficient communication media. This is because of the opportunity books give readers to go back and read the whole book or parts of it again. It is only quite recently that the electronic media offered the same opportunities through the use of cassettes, for instance.

To return to our observation of the world-reaching communicator, if he advocates a value system which is foreign to the political and religious creed that is his community's official faith and education, he becomes the communicator-abroad at the very moment he delivers his message to his own countrymen. Defacing synagogues may be a recognition signal among fascists and neo-Nazis in the United States, but its communicator is still the communicator-abroad no matter how American born he is, no matter how perfect his American English, because his native country is not a fascist state.

Another example of a communicator-abroad is, for instance, a Russian dissenter who spoke to hardline communists in the former Soviet Union about "freedom of speech." Freedom of speech was a foreign concept stemming from Western democratic value systems, but the dissenter at once becomes a communicator-at-home when he recommends the same concept of freedom, as glasnost paved the way for his message as a basic value in Gorbachev's USSR. If the Russian speaker tries to introduce the new concept of freedom of speech in the People's Republic of China, he is still a communicator-abroad, and this is not because of his Russian nationality. A bloody example of the communicator-abroad include the Chinese students who tried to convince the government with meetings and riots on Tiananmen Square in Beijing that democracy meant more participation by the common man in government and more free expression by the citizens.

But the models of communicators are not ironclad. Declarations of freedom and independence in the Baltic states, for instance, were faced by Russian communicators who, despite their talk about glasnost, immediately became communicators-abroad. This was not only because of the Russians' coming to the Baltic states, but because the Russians suddenly expressed their old ideology and attitudes when they fell back on their former imperial jargons and warned world opinion against "interference in domestic affairs," completely ignoring the Baltic struggle for independence from the USSR.

Another illustration is that of an American secretary of state speaking in Yugoslavia and calling for "territorial integrity." The meaning of his concept was at once interpreted by his deeply divided Yugoslavian audience as a sign of his support for the different sections of Yugoslavia in their violent fight for independence from each other. In fact, the American politician was speaking out from his own communication realm and meant "keep your whole nation intact" (Baker in Yugoslavia, July 3, 1991). In early negotiations between Arabs and Israelis, the call by an American mediator to "let us now sit down and discuss these problems as good Christians!" was disastrous—another example of the same parochial thinking.

The risk of becoming a communicator-abroad is not limited to speakers communicating with audiences around the globe. The United States itself gives daily examples of communicators-at-home and abroad. A Republican, for instance, talking to fellow

Republicans is at home if his audience shares his tenet, but is abroad if they are Democrats or Independents, just as a Democrat acquires the communicator-at-home label when speaking to fellow Democrats. As soon as the Democrat extends his message to Republicans or Independents, though, he at once becomes a communicator-abroad. We can only think of how *liberal* is used as a Janus-faced weapon in political campaigns between the two parties, its meaning far from the dictionary's.

The independent speaker is even more at risk than Republicans or Democrats in becoming a communicator-abroad among these two parties. He is in a no-man's land and has to look for other independents to become a communicator-at-home. This is not easy since the concept of independence often mirrors many states of mind. In fact, America as a nation often poses the same communication problems as the conversation with the whole global village with its different publics. The United States is not only fifty different states but often displays at least fifty states of mind and interests. President Lyndon Johnson complained bitterly of his Texas handicap when he tried to communicate with the rest of the country (K. Dovring, 1975).

Thus, the communicator's performance at home and abroad is of great importance if we want to understand the meanings of his words and concepts. It is summed up in the question to the communicator: "Who are you?" This is a question to answer not only for the professional analysts of his message, but not the least for his public's perceptions of his performance.

It should also be said here that the problems of communicator-at-home or abroad often comes up when the *establishment* tries to reach minorities inside or outside a nation, or when a member of the minority takes on the establishment. Religious movements and their adversaries have for centuries offered a fruitful area for research here. Their activity has not lessened in interest when religion turns into worldly politics, as it continues to do today in the Middle East or in Northern Ireland, for instance (K. Dovring, 1951; Lasswell, 1930). Language and its meanings are the coins of communication—just like money, it buys different things in different markets. Or, as Spanish-speaking farm workers in the United States said about a well-to-do, Spanish-speaking political candidate: He certainly speaks Spanish. But he does not speak *our* language. He was just another communicator-abroad.

We can hardly emphasize enough the importance of being aware of the roles of communicator-at-home and communicator-abroad and their different communication realms or circles. Originally, clearly separated by their basic doctrines and vocabularies, they had to overlap in various degrees when the communicator tried to get converts to his political or religious faith. The awareness of all this is the key to understanding public persuasions, their communicators, their obvious jargons and less obvious undercurrents, and their purposes. In both cases, the communicator-at-home and the communicator-abroad, there is a distortion of formal, accepted language, that is, of the languages of the official dictionaries and what we have learned as the proper use. The special ideology and purpose twists the official language and uses it for the communicator's goal. In extremist lingo, the distortion is quite obvious (K. Dovring, 1965a, 1965b, 1975). They overflow with colorful symbols. They create Lenin's special communication realm with his negative connotations of *capitalism, exploitation of the workers, imperial wars, child labor,* and *kulaks.* Then there are the positive concepts such as *socialism* and *correct policy* (correct is an often-used concept derived from Lenin's faith in "Correct scientific socialism"). Correct was then used *ad nauseam* in all kinds of contexts by his followers. Positive symbols also were the proletarian struggle, communist revolution, and so on. All are values that, by their continuous repetition and quantity, create the meaning and quality of his message and invite his public to join his special communication realm. The analysis of this has been called analysis by quantitative semantics.

In any country where Soviet communists appealed to the public, with success or not, in government and out of government, the Lenin concepts appear time and time again in communist speeches and talks. Eventually, ordinary words got a new meaning—the word *correct* for instance—by direction, manipulation, contexts, and by frequently repeated special uses that obliterate the original meaning the word once had in the established dictionary. As we said, President John Kennedy was exposed to this in his negotiations with the Russians, and lists were made on the bodysnatched English words. President de Gaulle had a similar experience in Moscow when he negotiated there and found a bodysnatched French that was unheard of in Paris and never had a chance to be approved by the Académie Française. This was another illustration of the bodysnatched language's international presence.

If the frequent uses of familiar words—but with a new meaning—are repeated often enough, they eventually create a special vocabulary and mirror a special creed. This is mostly observed in jargons of spectacular symbols. It can be seen the world over among youthful gangs of more or less criminal character. In the political arena we meet it in expressions such as "people's and workers' democracy," "peaceful coexistence," "objective laws of socialism," "breakdown of imperialism," "happiness of the masses," "capitalist roaders," "ideas of scientific communism," and "bourgeois exploitation," just to mention a few (K. Dovring, 1965a, 1965b). Sometimes the new meanings of the familiar words are indicated only by the negative or positive context and use of the concepts but always contrary to their accepted, familiar use in the dictionaries. For instance, capitalism is a positive symbol in the Western world, but is a negative concept in socialist doctrine. Democracy is a favorable idea in the West, but when Gorbachev (1986) used it, he pointed out that "Democratization means more Socialism."

Political communications are very rapid in their developments or changes of their misuse of a nation's familiar language or when their communicators handle a global lingua franca according to their own intentions. The jargon that is created reveals not only the nature and goals of the ideology behind the words and concepts, but it often gets outdated very quickly. This rather inspires the ideology and its communicator to form familiar words into new expressions of old thoughts while keeping the hard core of the fundamental doctrine intact. This also has the alarming side effect for the communicator that there is nothing so old and empty as yesterday's slogans. For instance, who gets upset nowadays by hearing calls for "Down with the Kaiser"? There may even be people who have no idea what Kaiser refers to.

As we have mentioned, the modern electronic media's global

reach and the stirring up of world opinion have made the extreme jargon more or less obsolete as communicators want contact with the vast audiences of today. Not even a dictator nowadays is free to choose his audience. He can always count on the fact that the world is listening, but just as important, he is in fierce competition and communication with other political and religious leaders because of the power of the global media. Therefore he is not only talking to audiences at home and abroad at the same time, but he is also communicating with other leaders around the world. He is truly in a no man's land. Power over communication is the base for his whole political or religious power at home and abroad. Power over communication is the last thing a dictator can let go. That is, he can never let it go. If he does, he is no longer in supreme control. This is an experience that is not limited to a dictator's struggle for influence and domination. Influence on public opinion rests on communication, which in turn is preparation for action or nonaction in social and political life.

Today, if anyone would care to listen to a dictator and the dictator wants to get his message across, like everybody else he has to soften his speech, cut out or reduce the extremist lingo, and put on a public relations guise. For instance, in the strife caused by the last communist dictator in Czechoslovakia before a democratic government took over, he had to soften his speech. At the same time, the journalists observed that behind the "soft speech" were still the same communist ideals. This ostensible cooperation was the only way the dictator could try to reach his own nation's increasing multitude of opponents and get into contact or exchange with outsiders, leaders, and publics of some other political faith and policy. This asks for both artistic skill and, above all, creativity, which can shape worlds of illusions and feelings of contact in public relations. The communicator cannot dictate anymore. At the same time, as we saw from the Czech example, the dictator today must see to it that he does not lose his own hardline ideological home public—wherever it is— and must retain the foundation of his power base. The current competition among leaders in the Russian Federation gives many examples of this volatile subject. Anyway, the communicator in this situation still manages to throw in one or two colorful ideological symbols, such as *imperialist* or *warmonger*, to reassure his old true believers longing for times past.

We shall see in later examples from the communicator's contacts and conversations that this is not the only tool he uses to enable his true followers to still feel at home and keep the faith; this despite his new approach to communication. In the balance between his use of the few explicit old symbols and of ordinary words that cunningly amount to the same symbols' meaning, and by artful repetition, he creates undercurrents of meaning that gratify his followers and often persuade or deceive his opponents. He is so convincing that he can make even the indifferent believe that the leopard has changed his spots. Of course, he runs a serious risk by softening his obvious jargon and its influence, especially if he completely omits the ideological recognition signals. He might even eventually become a victim of the new persuasion himself.

His use of ordinary language approved by the official dictionaries seems on the surface to work on cross-purposes in his communications. Both his followers and the outsiders and his opponents easily get confused by this. The hardline, orthodox communicator has to hide his true colors. He must "go underground" by manipulating his old message into a seemingly innocuous or new character, or he has to change allegiance or purpose altogether. It is there the dissident emerges. In all cases today, the dictator has to not only soften his jargon, but he also has to approach the democratic pattern of style and balance. He has to pay a lot of attention to the practical facts involved in an issue. A former Ku Klux Klan leader or white supremacist concentrates on the day's economic problems, for instance, in his speeches, but is silent about or apologizes for his past. Only an analysis of how he deals with the community values in addressing these economic facts will reveal his true political and philosophical identity and his psychological attitude (K. Dovring, 1959).

The democratic pattern of communication—stress on facts at the expense of ideology—is on the surface a message that embraces competing ideas in a debate. It is not enough anymore with ideological symbols chanted at the expense of concern for the facts. We shall later see in more detail how Gorbachev was only one example of just such a communicator. He became a revolutionary who faced the needs of our time by appealing to both his worldwide public and to his own nation as a public relations man.

Gorbachev himself is said to have summed this up after his first meeting with his American counterpart by saying: "I am no simpleton." This was a clear invitation to look carefully into his speech to discover the undercurrents of his meanings in his seemingly easygoing democratic style.

It is in this modern lingua franca we meet the most skillful double talk, the bodysnatched language, and covert propaganda. It is here we face the global use of trans-English since the modern electronic network has been the outcome of Western Anglo-Saxon supremacy. English has therefore become a lingua franca to be used and distorted by the world and its political and religious cross-currents. Awareness of this is needed more than ever in this age of mass movements for democracy, for freedom and nationalism *versus* the struggling leftovers of authoritarian regimes. It is here that it has become necessary to talk with a "forked tongue" since today's communicators are more than ever talking to and listened to by both the world and by people at home at the same time. These are two kinds of public that more often than not have different characters and are of different cultural age and ideological make-up. Therefore they interpret common words and concepts differently—when they have anything in common! Similarly, the same U.S. dollar, for instance, buys different things in different nations, and more or fewer things in one country than in another. The English language is a treasure of words used very differently in different parts of the world (Safire, 1991).

As another example, "law and order" spoken to a South African audience is understood differently both within the South African nation itself and the rest of the world. The skillful communicator must be creative enough to guide these varied interpretations according to his own meaning and purpose or, as some put it, distort for his own political goals. James Fenimore Cooper explained it very well:

> In short, he (the political communicator) so blended
> the warlike with the artful, the obvious with the ob-

scure, as to flatter the propensities of both parties, and to leave to each subject of hope, while either could say it clearly comprehended his intentions. The orator or the politician, who can produce such a state of things, is commonly popular with his contemporaries, however he may be treated by posterity (Cooper [1826], 1960).

More recent examples of this are political bank robberies being called "expropriations," or the murder of innocent, helpless hostages termed "legal execution" by the killers. The same expression was recently used by Nigeria's government when one of its opponents and outstanding poets was murdered by the authorities. Familiar words become loaded with new or partly new meanings that may influence and build up new attitudes with the unsuspecting public, often without its knowledge.

In a nutshell this also shows the situation of modern communications in today's worldwide dependence on electronic media and their opportunity to present well-known concepts with potentially different meanings. This calls not only for a common lingua franca on the surface, at home and abroad, but it also calls for skillful artists and actors, illusionists even, in communication. However, despite the calls for elegance, illusions, and efficiency in style and performance, all communicators today nevertheless have to deliver some substance in their message to their audience and to their competitors if they want to stay in power or to get power. Lenin, whose electronic communications were limited to gramophone records, did not realize this. He displayed the attitude of many public figures, past and present, when he brushed aside his associates' advice about the relation between facts and style in his messages. The main thing, he said, was to find concepts that could stir up public emotions before a certain fact. In *Mein Kampf* Hitler agrees wholly with Lenin here (Hitler [1925–27], 1934). For instance, speak to the mass public about technology and the issues surrounding "star wars" and only the experts will understand. Only when technology is presented in the ideological shroud of a means to avoid nuclear war, for instance, will the public rise to the occasion and understand. In short, concepts of social, ideological nature that are well known to the public had to be introduced and then dominate the substantial facts of nuclear technology. Only the social, emotional symbols would throw light on the facts and make them come alive to the public. This certainly made it easier for the communicator who is not always an expert on the issue himself when he tries to make it understandable to his mass public. Or take another example: The fact of nuclear power as a source of energy did not stir up the mass public before it was communicated in the light of mankind's survival, in war and peace, in sound environment, and by economic costs. AIDS attracted the mass public's attention first when it was pointed out as an incurable epidemic threatening everyone's health and life. Social concepts based in the community's ideology such as war or peace, health and environment, and mankind's or an individuals' death or survival made the scientific facts come alive. All these stirring, familiar concepts stemmed from our community ideology and could therefore popularize a difficult topic. But as we said, in our time, communicators must more and more give place to facts in their messages as the public gets more and more inquisitive. Lenin and Hitler did not face these demands. The public's quest for facts creates two interesting side effects. One is that the public must be willing to improve their education. The other is that the communicator must rely more and more on the undercurrents in his message when he wants to use the community values to draw the public into his fold. Understanding the scientific facts involved is still the prerogative of the scientists. They eventually had to deal with the result of this popularized communication of their specialty—another good reason for the scholars to take a close look at what happens to their scholarship in communications!

This popularization sometimes resulted in an often ignorant fear that clouded the public mind and made people easy prey for political purposes when the issue came up for debate by politicians and self-appointed moralists. The familiar words used in this popularization of facts, in the light of emotional social values, more often than not take on new meanings. This is one of the examples of Bodysnatched English. Another revealing illustration is the kind of public debate around the right to legal abortion. Community symbols such as "right to life" or "free choice" dominate discussions of medical facts that in themselves are controversial.

5

Listeners Beware: Infiltrators at Work

What can we as a public do to be aware of this bodysnatched communication? We can do just that, make ourselves aware of the process. We can go even further in understanding if we have the gift of analyzing what is happening. It is among those who have that gift that we can find the professional intelligence analysts—the analysts of propaganda, the communication experts, though not necessarily the scientific experts, on the topics that are in focus and up for public debate. However, as citizens most of us are served enough by being aware so we can maintain power over our own decisions when the communicator tries to inform us. Awareness means having a basic understanding of what is happening during communication, when familiar words are made to cover a new attitude, not always identical with our own interests or our educational background. That is, we have to look out when anything is popularized in information about events, scientific topics, or other news of interest to us. The damage may already be done when the pollster comes around and makes us statistics of the communicator's influence.

The communicators themselves have realized, of course, the powerful impact of the new language that seems to be proper and familiar on the surface as it relates to many substantial facts in the news or issues of today. The words seem to frame the news event in a very objective, unemotional, and informative way. We may be easily comforted when it is obvious from the context that we can detect whether the fact is put in a favorable or unfavorable light and whether this seems to agree with our preconceived ideas from our community education—or whether it is opposed to this. We therefore believe that we can make up our own minds and opinions on an issue without realizing that there may be repeated undercurrents of meaning in the communicator's handling of the facts being presented to us. This may get unexpected results. For instance, a communicator makes a glowing speech about "civil rights"; this is a positive concept in American society. But he may be a speaker who more often than not gets away with reducing the general symbol of civil rights into the opposite of civil rights by making it a cover word for "reverse discrimination," an ugly idea in American philosophy. How does he do it? Of course he mentions the words "civil rights" frequently. It is, after all, the topic of his speech. But very often the reference to civil rights is used in a close context of repeated references to alleged events where, for instance, white males have lost their jobs or been passed over for promotions in favor of minorities who may be less qualified for the job than the white male, but are preferred because a *quota* must be filled. By references to "quota" and "discrimination in reverse," the positive concept of civil rights is soon contaminated by a negative undercurrent. The message's sleeper effect then comes to the fore, even among those who believe they are free from any bias, as soon as someone feels that their own civil rights are being imposed upon. The concept has been tainted, and its meaning emerges as discrimination in reverse or quota—both used in a negative sense in later campaigns of propaganda. The concept's original philosophy and meaning, "civil rights for all," has turned into a qualified reference to double talk that could be used by all parties in the conflict. The process also illustrates the creation of Bodysnatched English. If the communicator had come right out in the beginning and talked about civil rights as discrimination in reverse, only those with an ax to grind would have become his sure audience. But by references to civil rights in general he reaches a large audience where everybody interprets the concepts "according to his own faculties," to quote James Fenimore Cooper once more, "since each one perceived that more was meant in the hidden meaning than was uttered" ([1826] 1960). Consequently, it was not surprising that the "management of Magua prevailed."

This semantic infiltration is, of course, something that does not only happen at home in domestic conversations. It is, as we know, not quite possible today to separate domestic and foreign communications because of the reach of the current media. This is another way of saying that the world is closing in on us. It is hard to see the difference in meaning of familiar words and concepts in the worldwide communication of modern times. Dorothy Thompson summed up the problem in a nutshell: She complained that no two people meant the same thing when, for instance, they tossed around the words *liberal* and *conservative.* An apt oberservation nowadays among politicians! She also observed that we do not even have a vocabulary that conveys semiprecise meanings (Kurth, 1990).

Fidel Castro used words that John Kennedy handled in *his* public diplomacy and conversations with the masses. The differences in meaning came out in the *balance* in the use of the same words and symbols. This balance revealed whether he was an authoritarian politician or a democrat of Western type. This gave different meanings to the same words. Mao Tse-tung talks in his *Thoughts* about "economic growth" as the ground for "equality" (K. Dovring, 1975; Bush, 1988). But the influence on the words' meanings that is created by the balance in a speaker's message and eventually reveals his political and psychological attitude is usually only obvious to professional analysts.

The same confusing surface similarity of public communications was also clear when Chile's then-president, Salvador Allende, seemed to communicate just like Lyndon Johnson in the United States (K. Dovring, 1975). In global communications, at home and abroad, there once emerged a sameness in the message that evoked suspicion and anxiety on both sides of the Iron Curtain. The Soviet Union's official newspaper of those days, *Pravda,* was at once ready to warn the public at home and abroad against the blandness in modern communications around the globe and the innocent-looking sameness in terms, words, and concepts when economic issues were discussed. This bland trans-English used as a lingua franca in conversation covered both

Western "imperialist influence" in socio-economic issues and "Chinese chauvinism," *Pravda* complained. But *Pravda* was not the only serious voice. The Soviet dissenters, long deeply sensitive to problems such as individual human rights, immediately warned the West not to accept "totalitarian standards" when it talked with the East. Totalitarian standards were just a reference to concepts from the ruling ideology that, by undercurrents of meaning, infiltrated the language and created attitudes among the public that made them consent to the communicator's purpose. Pope John XXIII, a professional diplomat sensitive to semantics, summed it up very well when he talked about "thought diffusion" (K. Dovring, 1965a, 1965b, 1975). An example of this emerged in a recent public discussion in New York when the state tried to rewrite its history books for use in schools and pointed out the need for "political correctness." One could also find the concept in American television news stories, referring to events as "politically correct" and even to "socially correct toys" (CBS News Report, December 8, 1991; Radio Broadcast, July 25, 1991, New York).

It was then reported from the Soviet Union on the same day as the news of the "correct policy" in the schools of New York, that the hardline communists, led by Gorbachev, vigorously rejected the ban on communist activity in the workplace, a ban imposed by Gorbachev's rival, the Russian president Boris Yeltsin. According to the hardliners, this ban was a violation of "freedom of speech," a symbol hardly at home in the hardliners' Leninist philosophy. But many times Gorbachev had the opportunity to face it among his Western admirers.

Earlier, the West Germans had complained about the Soviet occupation of East Germany and its "translation German" (Übersetzerdeutsch der Sovietzonalen Machthaber), a bodysnatched German the Soviets used in communication with their political satellites in East Germany in order to impose the Soviet's own standards of policy. Their communication was also an excellent example of the bodysnatched language's contempt and neglect of all kinds of normal grammatical and linguistic rules. In fact, it often appeared as a shorthand German or pidgin German deeply infiltrated with communist meanings from the Soviet communist jargons, but dressed in familiar German words, sometimes even using Russian grammatical rules (K. Dovring, 1965a).

On the other side of the globe, the People's Republic of China ordered its students of English to learn to "speak Chinese in foreign languages." That is, they should infiltrate ordinary English words by creating undercurrents of meaning from the Chinese communist creed so the global public opinion would be swayed in the communist direction, an order that had its risks, of course. It backfired at home, as we have mentioned, in the democratic uprising in Tiananmen Square in Beijing. Body-snatched English had arrived on a worldwide scale. The bloody catastrophe there gave the square a bad name that the People's Republic now desperately tries to turn into a concept of peace and happiness for China's children and visitors. In the American edition of the Beijing magazine *China Today* (October 10, 1996), the editors do their best to present in beautiful, colorful pictures and its best Madison Avenue–style "the charm of Tiananmen Square" as the heart of Beijing; "a wonderful place for sightseeing and play and display of sophisticated Chinese culture—a place that brings a smile to the faces of China's children." These attempts to create a new image fall flat considering the undercurrents of meaning the name got a few years back.

Bodysnatched language is not a new phenomenon. Christian missionaries through centuries have been forced to use semantic infiltration of the communication they used when they tried to make converts to their own faith and popularize and simplify difficult theological teaching. For instance, it was not always a simple matter of finding a replacement for the phrase "snow white." An African audience that never had seen any snow could not imagine what the missionary meant when talking about blood red sins that would be washed snow white through salvation. The missionary had to observe his audience's different communication realm and try to find a concept that was at least similar in meaning in his public's culture and physical environment.

But why go to Africa? In 1840 in New Bedford, Massachusetts, a preacher gave a sermon for the seamen who were going on a whaling ship. His comforting words of trusting in God who is our "rock of ages" could not be used as rocks were a danger to the sailors. They did, however, trust in the keel of the ship. Therefore "keel of ages" became the new religious symbol (Melville, 1851).

Some American scholars have insisted that identical concepts can be found in all cultures if one searches long enough. Obviously, they are mistaken. There are concepts that can never be translated because they don't exist in all communication realms across the world, as we have illustrated earlier. These exceptional concepts are native to their culture and exist only there, they have no analogues in other cultures. Anthropologists and speakers of foreign languages can confirm this.

The mission among non-Christian peoples was a challenge to communication at home and abroad, and to the gospel itself. The problem was to keep the original doctrine intact, but at the same time reach a foreign people steeped in their own religious cultures and mores. This turned out to be a very difficult process, and because of this the various Christian churches suffered many conflicts in their missions around the world. For instance, the Virgin Mary had to be presented in terms familiar and understandable to a people whose religious culture embraced a central, female goddess. At the same time, none of the Virgin Mary's essential features were supposed to be lost in the communication. This was a matter of balanced use of words and a careful direction of their meaning until the pagan goddess eventually took on the name and character of the Christian symbol. But this also posed the very real risk that some of the qualities of the pagan goddess would taint the Christian image in a public mind so long devoted to their own familiar divinity. So, the public's identification with the old goddess had to be moved to the new symbol and eventually dominate the image of their new faith. This made the road open for influencing the people into a crowd of converts to the new belief. Later, in the political arena, this process eased the way for women to be accepted by the people as powerful public leaders. Eva Peron was one of the most successful. She turned the process around and changed her people's devotion to the Virgin Mary into adoration of "Evita," the Savior of Argentina and its women.

Eventually, the Catholic missionaries became rather successful propagandists as they mastered the art of semantic infiltration of the foreign culture. To use the definition of propaganda: They manipulated symbols to control attitudes on controversial matters (Lasswell and Blumenstock, 1939). This mission was so essential to the Catholic church that it sponsored the missionary work by the Vatican's own special agency for communications around the world: The Congregatio de Propaganda Fide, in Rome.

Since religious missions often went hand in hand with geographical explorations around the globe, the political interests of various nations were not far behind in this missionary communication. Political doctrines often tried successfully to infiltrate the religious tidings by sending foreign policy signals in the undercurrents and implicit language of the message. Spain's Catholic missions through the centuries is only one of the many examples of this, and the Catholics had more challenges to face. The Protestants had their missions, too. There was the "Society for Promoting Christian Knowledge" (1698) and the "Society for Propagation of the Gospel" (1701), both based in Great Britain. On the continent in the eighteenth century, there were the German Pietists under the Reverend Francke and the Moravian Brethren under Count Zinzendorf. This competition added to everybody's problems in the non-Christian fields of communication.

There is an example, both domestic and international, from eighteenth-century Sweden and Germany that can be considered at some length here. It illustrates methods of communication from ages past that are still relevant in today's mass communication as it relates to any debate on issues that involve competing ideas on conflicting political purposes. It also gives us insight into details of the semantic infiltration when communication emerges as a struggle for power over minds and values. How the conflict was perceived, taught, and communicated showed that methods of dealing with it were not only useful in the eighteenth century, but turned out to be so basic for analysis of mass communication that they are still used in our time and are looked upon as the cardinal principle for propaganda analysis. This is true not only in times of war and extreme tension such as in the American analysis of fascist propaganda during World War II; the methods can also reveal the intentions of political leaders today who have strayed from authoritative communication to public relations' talk. To put it another way, these latter day leaders of nations prepare public opinion for action or nonaction on the national or international scene by their artful, creative conversations. As we know, public relations are a matter of cooperation with the public. This is a bold step from the authoritarian political communication where the leaders called the shots.

To return to the European example of the eighteenth century, Martin Luther's protestantism had become the state religion in Sweden, as in the rest of Scandinavia. After successful wars against mighty Catholic nations on the European continent—religious wars with political purposes—Sweden emerged as a great political power. However, not belonging to the "pure evangelical faith," as Luther's teaching was called, was tantamount to treason, political and religious, in Sweden. The great political-religious enemy was the Catholic faith and its Roman church. The Swedish state church—the well-financed, prolonged arm of the government—was in charge to ensure that every citizen, old, young, man, woman, and child, went to their neighborhood church every Sunday. Besides this, congregations were called at regular intervals to meet with the ministers of the church to face instruction and examinations in the Lutheran faith. Everything took place under the guidance of the church's ministers and with official approval of the government. Attending or holding private religious meetings in your home or elsewhere outside the church's jurisdiction was illegal and was punishable with heavy jail sentences.

Despite this vigilance, it was reported more and more frequently that secret religious meetings were taking place in people's homes. There they were singing hymns from songbooks not approved by the state censor, a powerful political watchdog at the time. The book used was one called *Songs of Zion*, first published in 1743 and reluctantly approved by the censor. He sensed something was amiss, but could not put his finger on it. The authors were anonymous, and the frustrated church authorities expressed their exasperation by telling anyone who wanted to listen that the book was "written by the Devil and printed in Hell." Even more alarming was the fact that the book was getting around not only in many later editions—illegally published—but also was distributed and used in manuscripts, a kind of early *samizdat*. The songs were filled with spectacular words whose frequent use seemed to create a special jargon that caused new public attitudes among the "ignorant mass," as the public was referred to at that time. In short, the words and concepts in the book smacked of new and foreign influence.

The orthodox clergy and the state at once detected heresy and rebellion. In fact, one could find words used in the book and then by the public from the dangerous Moravian sect in Germany whose leader, Count Zinzendorf, taught a confusing brew of catholicism and protestantism. He had declared that all religions were of equal value and that every person had human dignity. One of the "outrageous" consequences of this was that he even permitted women to preach. Just as alarming were the reports that certain young preachers in the protestant church—who were poorly paid and at the bottom of the clerical hierarchy—used words and concepts that seemed to create a new faith. Those new ideas could be found everywhere among the crowd in the street who had listened to these dubious ministers. It was obvious that the young Swedish preachers were communicators-abroad, even in their own country, from the Orthodox church's viewpoint, but were very much communicators-at-home among the dissenters influenced by the *Songs of Zion*.

All this loomed behind the political unrest that broke out all over the country among the "ignorant mass." People suddenly wanted to decide for themselves what they should think and believe. They opposed the king and thought of themselves as good as the king himself because they were taught by the dissenters' preachers that Christ had died for everybody, not only for the king. This was a dangerous teaching that, once transferred into the political and social arena, could upset the whole state hierarchy and kingdom, according to Sweden's attorney general at that time. The government and the church were worried. Something had to be done, and it was. The government sent out truth squads to the churches who discreetly listened in on the suspected ministers' sermons. The truth squads then listed and wrote down all words and concepts that sounded dubious and were frequently used, words that also had been heard among people in the street who were suspected of having listened to those preachers. The truth squads then submitted their lists to the church hierarchy and to the government for further action.

Not to be outwitted, the suspects and their followers made their own lists that attempted to prove that the "dubious words" listed by the truth squads were exactly the same words the orthodox preachers and official hymnals employed and were not only found in the *Songs of Zion*. So why was it right to use words such as Christ, blood, sins, and other familiar Christian concepts in the officially authorized hymnbooks but not in the *Songs of Zion?* Why, despite all the sameness in words, did the public react differently to the orthodox hymns and the *Songs of Zion?* Why, when an orthodox song appeared in the *Songs of Zion*, was it condemned with the others as proof of heresy and false communication? Did the orthodox words suddenly get another meaning through the "bad" company of the dissenters' songs? What kind of magic lingo was this? (K. Dovring, 1951).

Eventually, our own times came to face the same problems as those of the 1740s when familiar words such as *democracy, freedom*, and *self-determination* appeared in different media, context, and ideological and political cultures. However, after much scholarly discussion and acrimonious political debate among communication experts in the eighteenth century—carried out in their speeches, books, and pamphlets, not to mention the court appearances—the cardinal principles of propaganda analysis emerged. It was true, it was pointed out, that the same identical words and familiar concepts were used by the orthodox authorites and by dissenters. All of them used familiar concepts such as *cross, Christ, His blood, judgment, sin, love, salvation, God, mercy, punishment*, and so on. But it became evident that the use and timing of the words made a serious difference in the teaching of the orthodox ministers and the dissenters, and evoked quite different public replies and opinion on the same issue. Ultimately, the different use and context of the same words created a new character in the public's faith and a new attitude to spiritual and social life. So, lists were made—just as it was later done both in analysis of fascist broadcasting to the United States during World War II and in the Kennedy negotiations with the Soviets—to find out what the same words meant when used by adversaries locked in keen competition for the public mind or involved in high level negotiations. For instance, how many times was a word used in a message, and where? And when not used, when should it have been? If for the sake of argument one would say that words mean nothing, it was certainly sure that the attitudes they created meant so much more.

However, back in the eighteenth century, the orthodox faithful insisted that they were the ones who communicated the true, complete doctrine. They used all the Christian concepts during the whole year and emphasized some of them, such as Christ's suffering and love, but only at special times, such as Easter. But the dissenters talked about Christ's sufferings and love not only during Easter week, but were concerned with almost nothing else all year around. The result was that there was no place in their communication for Jehovah's ire and judgment and the sinners' repentance. The balance among the same words and concepts became lopsided and incomplete. Therefore a new teaching was created that was heretical and had religious and political side effects. So, there was one lesson in communication analysis! The same identical words and symbols got a different meaning by the balance in their appearance and context and by the frequency—or lack of it—they were used in a message, that is, how much they were used or not used and when and by whom. In short, the quantity of their semantics played havoc with their meanings and created a bodysnatched language.

Harold D. Lasswell, who was a pioneer in the analysis of this kind of communication, faced the problem early in his research on war communications and propaganda and in his surveys on which tools media are using to get the public's attention. He stressed from the beginning that an analyst of communicators and their messages must be well versed in the culture their media represented, as well as being familiar with their countries' histories. From this knowledge he picked what he proved were the key symbols of a country's communication. Then he counted the appearance of the cultural and political key symbols in the media, whether it was during war or peace. We have examples from this kind of research in his "world attention survey" on national and international leading newspapers and in his studies of the propagandists' communications during times of war. This approach to research is deeply integrated in all his principal works. In his studies of the public messages, he questioned what was brought to the public's attention in peace or war. However, he was fully aware that the simple counting of key symbols used in the media to get the public's attention only scratched the surface of a message even though the symbols were the signs that most people were aware of. He warned that there were undercurrents of meaning in the key symbols themselves that pointed to the real purpose of the message and that did not show up by this kind of research. What he found was the frequency or lack of it in the key symbols' appearance. One could conclude from this research, however, that if more attention to the key symbols was displayed by the message, such as *democracy*, this indicated increasing importance of the concept in the public debate. If the concept began to occur less frequently, that meant that the communicator wanted to pave a new way to lead the public's awareness away from democracy. Then came the important question of the meaning of democracy for the different publics and communicators, and not the least for the analyst himself; he had to ignore his own opinion on what democracy should mean when he observed the communicators' performance. Here the question of ideological undercurrents came in and, as we said, was not revealed by a simple counting of symbols.

The frequency of the use of the key symbols pointed to times of crises and wars. Less frequency mirrored a calmer political climate and forecast more normal times. These surveys over the media's use of key symbols, in messages at home and abroad, made Lasswell conclude that this use was not only a matter of style; it was also sensitive to and revealed the currents in democratic society that were moving away from democracy. The same kind of analysis could, of course, also detect drifts toward democracy in authoritarian communities. Lasswell shows examples of this from newsmedia in both fascist Germany and Stalinist Russia and its reluctant satellites. But the examples are increasing in our time, in both the few remaining authoritarian nations' media and in the struggling countries newly freed from totalitarian chains.

This observation of the vagaries of attention to relevant concepts created, among other things, Lasswell's analysis of war propaganda during World War II. The results were used by the U.S. Department of Justice as legal evidence against communicators suspected of disloyalty by their use of fascist symbols in media and conversations. His analysis also gave birth to the Hoover studies on national and international leading newspapers from the past and his own time. There were also analyses of slogans from the Soviet Union (Lasswell, Lerner, and Pool, 1952; Pool et al., 1951, 1952). Lasswell got many followers among intelligence analysts in various countries and by studies in scholarly agencies and periodicals (K. Dovring, 1967).

Advanced scholars from emerging countries were more attentive in general to this kind of research than were some Westerners, especially the Americans who often lived up to Mark Twain's description of "innocents abroad." People from the Third World often were extremely aware of the difference between being "at home" and "abroad" in their communications. Americans preferred to believe that their "at home" was everybody's "at home." Often they failed to understand how "abroad" they really were.

The emerging countries' quick understanding of the problems was to be expected, since they were often in the middle of the practical consequences of persuasive political communications among their own leaders and foreign politicians and daily they tasted the bitter fruit of a communication that vacillated between Western democratic ideas and authoritarian policy.

However, the basic problem facing them was the same as that with the Swedish and German analysts in the eighteenth century: Why do the same identical words and concepts evoke different public attitudes and responses so as to make the public and individuals become polarized into government faithful *versus* dangerous dissenters? Or as the Scottish poet Robert Louis Stevenson put it when he traveled across the United States at the end of the nineteenth century: "They were speaking English all about me, but I know I was in a foreign land . . . For although two nations use the same words and read the same books, intercourse is not conducted by the dictionary. The business of life is not carried out by words, but in phrases, each with a special and almost a slang signification . . . Thus every difference of habit modifies the spoken tongue . . ." (Stevenson, [1883] 1966). It seems to be an eternal problem: How do words and concepts clearly identical in appearance and meaning to the members of one circle, be it the eighteenth-century Moravian Brethren or the Orthodox clergy or today's Western democracies *versus* totalitarian ideologies, acquire undercurrents of new meanings when the same words and concepts are used? Not only that, but the identical words and symbols might create different attitudes and opinions among both those belonging to the different circles or communication realms and the outsiders. Among these opinions one could find both opposition to the ruling government, or dissenters conscious of their attitude (or not), or faithful followers to the ruling government.

The answer to the puzzle was in the undercurrents themselves, which were created by the different uses of identical words and symbols. Even though the eighteenth-century scholars and politicians were only groping their way to this insight, they nevertheless had to confront the practical consequences for public opinion. Then, as now, the different uses of identical key symbols such as "democracy" or "selfdetermination" or "peace in our time," for instance, got undercurrents of meaning by *who* used it, *how*, and *when* it was used, the context in *which* it applied, and to *whom* it was said. And then there was the *effect*, which became different depending on whether the audience was made up of followers, dissenters, or just people out for a stroll, open to all kinds of influence. The famous Lasswellian formula, "Who says what to whom and with what effect?" sums up any communication performance. No wonder that the mere counting of key symbols in the media of yesterday and today could only touch the surface of a message; its importance was in the fact that it presented the attention area that was obvious to the mass public. People could easily recognize familiar symbols such as "sweet home" or "Benedict Arnold," and reacted in a positive or negative way, depending on the light these symbols spread on social circumstances and on facts that were up for debate.

The opponents of such analysis were ready to point out that there were sections of the message that never became analyzed, suddenly forgetting about the widely accepted use of sampling in scientific research. As we said before, the mere counting of the appearance of key symbols explained what was likely to catch the public's attention. This result was lost on the critics who insisted that a message should be analyzed in detail from all aspects. This—telling it all—was an enterprise that neither the public's education nor the news media had time or space for. The fact is that observation of key symbols also explores the effects already present in their character. The news media themselves rely very much on the character of key symbols when time and space force them to present the day's news and events in short order. A society's key symbols—explicitly mentioned or only taken for granted as an undercurrent—lighten the public's attention to a factual piece of news. "The President is shot" is an extreme illustration of this. But if the flow of information stops at the media's attention calling, the public is no better off than the mass public in medieval times who got their information from the pictures in the *Biblia Pauperum*. Edward R. Murrow, in his wartime broadcast from London, illustrated this in his frequent use of key symbols. Later, during both the cold war and current unstable times, American television gives many examples of the use of key symbols in their programs (Powers, 1977). The process has its ultimate fulfillment in messages of propaganda, be they political, commercial, or religious.

Harold Lasswell also explained that this kind of content analysis, which merely concentrated on observation of key symbols in a message, was a deliberate simplification that lost some of the message's rich double meanings, or double-entendre, just as the public's reaction did. At the same time, he emphasized that any artist—the ideal communicator—realized in his work the extraordinary economy by which meanings can be communicated by key symbols. This is well known to every artist, and it can also be said of any successful communicator and propagandist. They use it enough to justify a counting of the key symbols they apply. Just take a look at the many successful slogans in political and commercial life!

The history of communications, politics, and the arts illustrates this to an overwhelming degree. Saint Birgitta, a fourteenth-century nun in Sweden, which was Catholic at that time, was an outstanding scholar. But she was also a very skillful communicator who early on discussed the difference between the experts and the public's limited ability to grasp a message. Time and time again she urged communicators to see to it that they entered the public's "level of understanding" (*begripelseförmåga*). The communicator could be an elitist at home but was often abroad among the mass public, just as the mass public could be at home in its own ideas but often faced a communicator who was abroad to his public in his background and purpose. One can just think of the long line of communicators: from the Old Testament's early prophets to the Vatican, to Lenin and Churchill, to Hitler and Peron, to the sales people and public relations stars on Madison Avenue, to the politician-magicians and religious evangelists in modern mass media, finally closing the circle at the ideologue Mikhail Gorbachev turning public relations man. All of them had or have now one great problem in common: how to enter the public's level of understanding. No wonder that many among them had to settle merely for arousing the public's *attention* and *interest* to get *influence*. *Understanding* was something to brush aside (K. Dovring, 1959). Lenin was not the only one who did this successfully.

The neglect of understanding, that is, what the message really was about, was something a communicator passed over at his own peril. The role of undercurrents in a message that was created by the balance of the meaning in the key symbols as they framed the facts in a message could play havoc and backfire, both among the public and communicators. Remember the different interpretations of a symbol such as "love" and its meanings and undercurrents. Harold Lasswell was keenly aware of this double or triple talk. Even so-called "universal symbols" are not static details of unchanging configurations, he explained. To quote de Toqueville: "In democracies people are apt to entertain unsettled ideas, and they require loose expressions to convey them" (de Toqueville, [1835] 1945). Lasswell also points out that the communicator's contact with the public is not only a matter of using words and phrases. The communicator as well as the analyst and an attentive public—which the public not always is—must be strongly aware of the inner meaning of these words and phrases in different communication realms. It is this insight into the practical reality of mass communications that made scholars all over the world take up the challenge from Lasswell and his associates who started their research on what was offered to the public's attention, even though they realized that the undercurrents in a message had consequences too important to be ignored in the long run.

6

Echo of Double Talk

Early in this book it was suggested that we take a look at Body-snatched English and how it may influence the meaning of words and concepts manipulated by the minds that are behind this influence peddling. We also said that the result of that manipulation was bound to show up in people's opinions and attitudes. Unfortunately, people were not always aware of what was happening. The previous chapters aimed at illustrating the framework in which Bodysnatched English can operate. Let us now finally catch a glimpse of how Bodysnatched English appears in a practical way.

We have hinted off and on to the well-known fact that mankind's history is not one of democracy in a Western sense. Political communication has more often than not taken on the form of different hierarchies talking *to* and not *with* their public. The ultimate expression of this communication is to be found among dictators of various persuasions. It is the dictators' patterns of communication that have dominated human history, not the public relations conversation. For instance, the *edict* of imperial Latin (that is, the emperor's will immediately became law) was translated directly into the *ukaz* of imperial Russian. And in Chinese imperial symbolism, the gesture of *kow-tow* (kneeling deeply before the emperor and touching the ground with one's forehead) represented the extreme acceptance of the authority of the emperor.

One of the United States' great achievements—which seldom, if ever, is mentioned—is that it strives to be a creative pioneer in communications of Western democratic type where the public and rulers share the platform, and communication is a two-way street. To quote president Lyndon Johnson: "Let us reason!" Another aspect of this is the U.S. mission in the world as a model of freedom. This ambition is reason enough to explain its failure in being an efficient policeman for the world.

Only recently has the world seen a ruler from an authoritarian state successfully break hierarchial communications and try to debate with the public on a more or less equal basis. Let us first see what kind of old authoritarian pattern he had to abandon and then how he advanced from the chains of ideology to what appeared to be a debate on mere facts.

Examples from authoritarian communications dominate history. And when we say *authoritarian* we also mean totalitarian. Some scholars-turned-diplomats insist that there is a difference. There is a problem in accepting this. Argentina was called an authoritarian state, but it murdered tens of thousands of its citizens without even a trial.

What kind of communication did a dissident use to get into contact with the Western democracies of today and with the emerging nations who strove for freedom in the Western sense? Let us first see what kind of lingua franca the dictators used with their people and the rest of the world, because it is from this background that we have to look at the Bodysnatched English as a lingua franca of today's world. As is well known, the dictators often ruled in countries where individual freedom was denied, and consequently freedom of speech was also denied. The rulers dictated to their people, and the political doctrine formed the lingo. As Boris Yeltsin, the new president of the Russian Federation, said: "After Brezhnev, any leader of the Soviet Union who could speak 'normally' was looked upon as a hero" (Yeltsin, 1990). Only disastrous economic conditions made it necessary to try another kind of rule and communication.

John XXIII, pope and professional diplomat, stated in his encyclical of 1961 that the root of so much distrust among nations was their different ideologies. Therefore, he continued, people cannot hope to come to open and full agreement on vital issues. For instance, both sides speak about "justice" and "the demands for justice," but the words frequently take on different or opposite meanings according to which side uses them. When rulers of nations appeal to justice and the demands for justice, they don't only disagree on terms, but often increase the tension between their states (K. Dovring, 1965a, 1965b).

History and current events tend to confirm this frank recognition of the political role of semantics and ideologies in international relations and in today's domestic conversations—two fields that are closely intertwined thanks to electronic technology. One recent example is Saddam Hussein, ruler of Iraq, who expressed his joy during the attempt to topple President Gorbachev. It was, said Hussein, an event of "correct international balance," and he also insisted on calling the international hostages he had taken "guests" in his country. Meanwhile he took cover by accusing his enemies of "semantic misunderstanding" in their translations. One can here recall Esaias Tegner's exasperation about the translator or the interpreter as the biggest "traitor" of all.

How did the old, strictly doctrinaire communications look in choice of words, balance of themes and interest, and open or covert purpose? How did the new age of communication, as represented by Gorbachev, sway both his own home public and world opinion? Nobody can deny his pioneer work, whatever his position was or later may become. Can we get a picture of his performances by looking at his use of obvious trans-English or bodysnatched language in his talk? And then can we compare this with his predecessors' authoritarian rantings and their sharp contrast to the current use of plain English with covered undercurrents in meanings? Let us try.

From Lenin to the Vatican, from Hitler to Eva Peron, from Mao Tse-tung to Fidel Castro and other rulers of various creeds, and from self-styled zealots on single political-moral issues, the world has been made familiar with totalitarian or authoritarian communications. What has been good or evil for mankind is not the issue here. What we try to do is to clarify the patterns of communication used by rulers and zealots. Without knowledge we cannot make up our minds and be free from the grasp of the communicator's catch. To know where we are going is of increasing importance in today's world and its conversations in lingua franca.

To give a few examples: How did the hardline communists, bent on world revolution, communicate? Boring! It is the world opinion's catchword for it nowadays. Nevertheless, the world had to live with it up till now. Those people within nations ruled by totalitarian dictators eventually became skilled in double talk themselves when people spoke with each other or with strangers. All words became suspect, to quote Vladimir Sorokin (Sorokin, 1985). They became a tragic illustration of the same wit, humor, and sarcasm which was once a delightful conversation in peaceful Gothenburg, which was mentioned earlier.

The character of authoritarian communication is the special vocabulary, easy to distinguish and react to—whether agreeing with it or opposing it. Worldwide samples of authoritarian communications that were done some years ago studied documents from the famous Vatican labor-relations encyclical of 1891 to later Vatican messages, including some of its political faithful followers, as well as fascist imitators such as Eva Peron. Lenin and his Leninist-Stalinist successors among political rulers and their later supporters were also analyzed together with legislation inspired by the two different camps. The communicators all wanted to discuss solutions to economic problems and labor relations of their time. However, more often than not, their ideological framework dominated not only their speeches and vocabulary but also prescribed their creed's capacity as the solution to socioeconomic problems. The ideology became the remedy for social ills. This remedy was expressed with colorful ideological symbols and words, repeated time and again at the expense of references to the economic issue that was said to be the topic for debate. So the "workers democracy" had to be built only by "the objective laws of Socialism." In the Catholic camp, overpopulation was a great problem, but the "drastic policy of birth control" was an absolutely forbidden solution. The Vatican excelled in religious-moral concepts such as the "authority of God and Church" and its social teaching, or "moral justice" and concern for "man as a social individual." "Right to private property" was also emphasized in condemnation of "socialists," "greedy capitalists," and "injustice." All these ideological concepts dominated messages from the Vatican as well as heavily influencing members of governments strongly leaning toward Catholic teaching, such as the Democrazia Cristiana Party in Italy. Attention to the practical issue was less than to ideological symbols. All suggestions for solutions to social problems were tainted by ideological concepts. The messages became an act of guidance, not a solution to the socioeconomic troubles. The public hardly needed to be attentive to be able to see where the message came from. However, the indoctrination of the public did not stop with the use of colorful symbols at the expense of facts. If one carefully observed the message one could see that the ideological symbols, spectacular as they were, were surrounded by familiar words that were used as synonyms for the ideological concepts. This strengthened even more the power of the ideology and gave undercurrents of new meanings to words that did not have this quality originally. For instance, "justice"— a positive concept—became "rights of God in society." This concept was closely connected with "right to property"—later presented to the world as a basic Christian concept—just as "family" and "paternal authority" paved the way for "state authority" and "lawful order." These were all presented as positive synonyms to clearly clerical symbols. Highly negative were the ideas of "proletariat," "socialism," "injustice," and "birth control," all expressed in contexts that presented them as a menace to the church. Already by this time the bodysnatched language was at work. But the Vatican's messages are not only a repetitious indoctrination of clerical symbols guiding or dominating a social issue. The important point is also made in the communications that it is "false to believe that economic science and moral discipline should be kept separated." This is a clear justification from the Vatican's point of view for its concern about secular affairs.

"Who said it?" of course plays a significant role in authoritarian communications as well. The very balance between ideological concepts and hard facts in a speech or picture reveals whether the communicator is an authoritarian or something else. All the Vatican messages (and its political followers and imitators) in the study strongly emphasized ideological symbols at the expense of facts. Thus, the speaker was more interested in his ideological platform and power than in the factual topic he was supposed to handle. Furthermore, the emphasis on the ideology being communicated to the public made the speaker appear a very strong authority who was very optimistic in his approach to social problems. But the truth was that if one analyzed how the powerful symbols were used, whether in a positive or negative vein, the communicator who tried to display an image of strength often came down as a weakened ruler by the undercurrents that came through in his handling of the symbols that identified his power. Also revealing is a communicator's use of symbols when he sets his eye on his opposition or his open enemies. The authoritarian communicator does not give his audience a strong image of his opposition. Usually, he tries to ignore it more or less, but a look at the references to it, can clearly reveal how he uses more or less derogatory concepts in his description of his adversaries; the more derogatory, the more nervous he is. He also may give patronizing attention to his enemies in arrogant self-deception or self-reliance. His performance is an indication of his real strength or weakness. Finally, all his symbols build up the themes in his message. More often than not the power of authority the communicator claims to have is the main theme of his message if he is totalitarian. The social or economic issue that is up for debate usually has a hard time competing with his interest in consolidating the power of his ideology to solve, for instance, practical economic problems. The more critical a time is—war or cold war, economic disasters, or national or international tension in general—the more emphasis is laid on community ideology. The emphasis on ideological authority instead of facts is typical of these kinds of communicators and their political followers and imitators, such as the fascist extremist Eva Peron, who don't hesitate to use the clerical authoritarian pattern of communication for their own political totalitarian purposes.

Lenin, his followers, and the Stalinists are no exception to the totalitarian patterns of communication despite their doctrine, which is opposite in all regards to that of the Vatican and its followers. There is the same emphasis on authority whether they call it the state or the people or the party. The jargon is just as repetitious and ideological, the demands for change and revolution are just as optimistic on the surface. But this optimism disappears when the adversaries are bitterly and derogatorily referred to. The intensity of the negative references increases the more insecure the situation is. Lenin himself was revealed to be on very shaky ground, and this situation improved only when the revolution was a success as in Khrushchev's speeches.

However, a new time is coming. Immediately after World War II there were signs of a new pattern of communication. The French socialist government in 1945, which faced social unrest and economic disaster in their war-torn country, is an early example. Even though the government's spokesperson may show strong confidence in his power, his demands for reform are solely concentrated on the economic facts when he meets his public. The opposition is noted but with emphasis more on social ills than on hostile opponents. The ideological lingo is restrained, and more and more everyday words are used that increasingly get their undercurrents from the topical character of the issue under debate rather than from ideology. But it can also be observed that these undercurrents do not always take their meaning from the facts of the economic issue that is discussed, for instance. All undercurrents can be influenced by both facts and ideology, and they sometimes were, as in the French example of the new communication. It has often been argued that no communicator can be absolutely free from his own ideological past; either he still identifies with it or insists that he is free from it. Again the question of balance comes up.

This new trend in communication was taken up by the Vatican of John XXIII and his followers and by Khrushchev, among others. It also became the pattern for John Kennedy and other democratic leaders of the West, not to forget about communist hardliners such as Fidel Castro (with a slip-up here and there!). Castro, however, has quite another kind of undercurrent of meaning when he uses the new democratic pattern he has borrowed from his Western contemporaries. He is democratic on the surface since he talks to both his public at home and world opinion and is in keen competition with the communicators of the Western world at the same time. Only occasionally does Castro return to the old vocabularies of the hardline communist leaders and mixes in the ideological jargon with his seemingly innocuous communication. This throwback to the old pattern of communication comes readily to the fore the more embittered he gets. Despite his resistance, however, the time has come for a more consciously Bodysnatched English—or as the rulers of the People's Republic of China phrased it: to speak Chinese in foreign languages.

Difficult economic problems and the emergence of world opinion through the electronic media set the stage for a radical break with the ideological jargon. And the authorities in all countries increasingly often had to face growing public opinion that questioned their power. In the United States people started to hate their politicians (Dionne, 1991), and local reporters showed a better grasp of the state of the union than the established journalists in Washington (Gary Hart in discussion with political campaign managers, January 1991, PBS, TV). In the rest of the world, public opinion often started its own revolution and uprising against the political authority.

Among the pioneers in this new opposition against authority is Mikhail Gorbachev. Here is a case where the ideologue turned into a public relations man. It became a case where the new art of communication eventually overtook its user with unforeseen political consequences for both himself and his nation as well as the rest of the world. In the arena of political communication, this was just as shattering an experience as the other revolution of 1991 in the Soviet Union. The relative openness to the press and to television and radio broadcasting was only one side of the process. The focus in the beginning was on Gorbachev himself, a conspicuous and successful Leninist who gave the appearance of a shrewd, sympathetic public relations man. He was, however, not followed by everybody. He was not the first one who tried to throw off the chains of ideology in communications either. Before him there were, as we remember, other speakers who tried to pay less attention to their ideological ties and show more concern for facts. Among them were not only the socialist French government in 1945, but also Chilean president Salvador Allende in 1972. Meanwhile in the United States, the Western pattern of communication flourished. John Kennedy, Lyndon

Johnson, Richard Nixon, Gerald Ford, Jimmy Carter, Ronald Reagan, George Bush, Michael Dukakis, and Bill Clinton all showed a balance between authority and facts that made their conversations a firm contact with their public. It was true, of course, that the time when a speech was made influenced the speaker and made him look at himself, at the demands he made, and the opposition he noted. One could see that certain psychological features were missing from their undercurrents. The democratic pattern of communication, free from obvious ideology, was used all the time by the various speakers. All of them talked *with* the public about facts, or tried to do so. The balance in this changed more or less with the individual speaker and created his image and the purpose of his message with the undercurrents. Some of them moved close to an image of a potential dictator, others kept close to their public's interests and concentrated on the topical facts in their speeches. And as usual in a democracy, its character of controversy and diversity gave people the chance to choose among the different leaders.

Martin Luther King Jr. was no exception to the democratic pattern of communication, but his undercurrents gave him a special place among contemporary politicians. The undercurrents in his concepts were very optimistic—an attitude that was all the more remarkable since his message was delivered from his jail cell in Alabama.

An early case of Bodysnatched English was that of a traveler in Hungary after World War II who tried to cover his communist alliance in familiar English words when he spoke to his countrymen and the world. But the undercurrents of his meanings for these familiar words were inspired by his communist faith, and the balance in their use showed his psychological and political character and allegiance.[1]

The art of authoritative communication had trouble in relinquishing its power. The crises in the Middle East, for instance, in the 1980s and 1990s created throwbacks to political and religious patterns of communications that were in full compliance with the most traditional acts among dictators laden with ideologies. The dictators were still talking *to* their people and to captive audiences at home and abroad. They did not talk *with* them. In light of this throwback, our time's new art of communication and political public relations may get a more obvious profile.

Economic issues have usually been in the center of political conversations no matter what topic was in focus. It is in our time that the economic and controversial issues first got a chance to join forces with the emerging world opinion—at home and abroad. This common global need could not be expressed without the modern electronic media. Together they have forced open the frontiers of many nations and cultures across the globe and contributed to the awareness of a world economy and its challenges to different nations and cultures.

We have pointed out before that this access across the borders was not always looked upon by everyone as a blessing. Some nations accused others of dominating the airwaves and therefore holding power over other nations' political, social, and cultural lives. Recently, for instance, Japan announced plans for a global network that would reach at least Asia and Africa, in fact a kind of Voice of Japan. In what language or languages? One thing is certain: Bodysnatched language will appear, no matter in which tongue the news or event is broadcast. A global communication language will certainly carry strong undercurrents of biased use in accord with the political and social culture that sponsors the broadcasting network. Since we live in a time of "mergers and take-overs," no national cultural centers will be immune from foreign influence. That this influence often becomes a two-way street is interesting.

NOTE

1. Research on communicators and their messages in the United States and abroad is reported in part in K. Dovring 1965b and 1975. For methods, see K. Dovring 1965b. More recent documents have also been analyzed in detail as indicated earlier in this book.

7

Lunch and Dinner at the Kremlin

Both present and past times of stress and tension, during peace or war, always have their own way of communicating with the masses and the rulers of nations. But in the 1980s a new deal worked its way up in human and political contacts. The president of the Soviet Union, Mikhail Gorbachev was a conspicuous and successful pioneering example of the new time: the ideologue turning deliberately into a shrewd public relations man and salesman. He was certainly not followed by everybody, as later events confirmed, and neither was he the first to deliver facts without obvious ideology, as we mentioned. But the communicators of different nations who forecast his pattern of communications were of less consequence than the new voice from Moscow, if one looks at it from a global viewpoint.

When Gorbachev of the Soviet Union hit the world market with his new brand of communism in communication, the Western world was stunned. Even his body language was different from his predecessors in the Kremlin. He mixed with enthusiastic crowds; his smiles and handshakes with people in the street became important undercurrents in his message, as did the appearance of his wife, Raisa, an expert on Leninist doctrine, elegant and well dressed, arm in arm with her husband. Already this was a step from the obscure oblivion that had been the usual place of the spouses of Russian dignitaries. One Western politician expressed more than astonishment when she said that Gorbachev was a man one could do business with. In fact, she expressed a general feeling in the West.

What was it in Gorbachev's communication that made people the world over sit up and listen and, above all, hope? Mutual business assumes some kind of meeting of minds and consideration of both parties involved, or the several parties involved—in short, some kind of public relations. The prerequisite for this is that a closed door is being opened. Even though only a thin ray of light comes through the open door, this sign of future light might fascinate and sometimes blind those unaware of the character of the glasnost that comes through. The impact of the human voice coming out of an unknown fortress so threateningly silent for so many years also startles and gives hope.

How did Gorbachev do it? How does an ideologue turn into a public relations man and sell his ideas through his communication and performance? Let us take a look.

Early signs of his new approach came in 1985 when he published a book in the United States. He called it *A Time for Peace.* The subtitle on the cover tells us that the author is a person who has taken some lessons from Madison Avenue and its thinking; it reads: "The Only Edition of this Book World Wide." This is a fact that many hopeful authors have painfully shared after publishing! The author also warns that he has the sole right for his work, come what may. This invites us to think that he may have something in common with his American capitalist-minded public and its strong desire for profit. Nevertheless, it is the ruler of a communist empire who speaks.

His book is composed of five speeches that Gorbachev made during the years 1983–85. The places where the speeches were delivered and the occasions at which they were given suggest something new. We are meeting a politician from a formerly tightly closed society that is beginning to display wide interests both at home and to the rest of the world.

The first speech, on April 2, 1983, is aimed at the Soviet home public and faithful communists abroad. It is about "Leninism as a Living and Creative Science. A Faithful Guide to Action" (cf. F. Dovring, *Leninism: Political Economy as Pseudoscience,* 1996).

This guideline to Leninism was presented by Gorbachev at a meeting in Moscow to mark the 113th anniversary of Lenin's birth. Another speech, delivered on December 10, 1985, is also aimed at the Soviet people. It is called "Creative Effort of the People." Formally, it is a report to the "All Union Scientific and Practical Conference" in Moscow. It does not only pay homage to the Soviet people, but it is also noted in Gorbachev's book that the speech is of "great significance" and has therefore been included in his book.

A third speech that also is promoted because of its great significance, finds Gorbachev in London, where he charms the British parliament on December 18, 1984.

After traveling to the West, he plays graceful host in the Kremlin to two international guests of state. On May 21, 1985, he entertains the then–prime minister of India, Rajiv Gandhi, with a dinner speech. At a lunch in the same palace one week later, on May 27th, Willy Brandt, leader of the German Social Democratic Party and president of the Socialist International, gets the same kind of entertainment.

The first speech, "Leninism: A Living and Creative Science. A Faithful Guide to Action," is a commitment to guide faithfully the public to the idea that Leninism is "a living and creative science." "Science" as the term for communist ideology is one of the basic concepts in Lenin's teaching. "Living and creative" indicates that the speaker knows he has to face reality and must look for "new ways to put the old wine in new bottles." In the book itself the speech also has the title "To Protect Peace," which can be taken as a goal of the speaker.

In what psychological and political situation was Gorbachev at that time? He was new in his position and represented a younger generation than his predecessors. His country was suffering from serious economic problems and from a war in Afghanistan that exhausted both human and financial resources. Still around him were many of the old politicians and *apparatchiki* just as reluctant to reform as the political bureaucracy whose self-interest was the status quo.

He also had to consider a public of fellow communists at home and abroad that was used to a dictator's ranting and repetition of old concepts and slogans. Then, but not least, there was the underground of dissenters and the doubting Western public and world opinion. However, in this speech, he above all has to appear as the communicator-at-home if he is to succeed in beginning a new era of reform and openness in his country and its political satellites. So his—and hopefully his public's—*attention* is concerned with old reliable concepts from Lenin's teaching. This is something everybody can observe. All communists are made to feel at home with the many references that identify them as "comrades" or point to "Lenin," "socialism means peace," "peaceful co-existence," and so on. But these clear communist symbols of identification (48.6% of the message's concepts) are smartly overpowered by the remaining (51.4%) references to such facts as "reduction of arms," "avert nuclear war," "building up national economy on democratic basis,"—the last reference a two-faced concept since here, as in several other instances, the ideological undercurrent, "democratic," is closing in on the economic problem and results in bodysnatched language.

It is evident that this balance between ideology and facts cannot assure that either side wins in the battle for his loyalty. Here he enters public relations as a seemingly loyal believer in the official Leninist doctrine. After all, the speech was delivered in the Soviet Union of the early 1980s.

However, on the topic of reforms, he seems to show little concern for his ideology. Only 19.7 percent of the references to reforms include clear ideological symbols such as "our party," "the Lode Star" (the famous emblem on the Soviet Union's flag), "points to the way of the future of international relations," and "disarmament a means for the further development of the Leninist principles," while no less than 80.3 percent call for detente and universal security *but* "according to Leninist principles of peaceful coexistence." Here as earlier, the ideological concepts come up in the undercurrent of his talk and taint the practical issue—disarmament and the future of international relations. This also makes the meaning of the concepts a victim of bodysnatched language. Practical demands are made within the context of the weakened ideology, but it exists there nevertheless. Gorbachev had obviously begun a new way of communicating. He slowly tried to free himself from the expressions of rigid doctrine and emerged as a public relations man among his fellow communists. At the same time, he appealed to both the old faith and to the practical problems of his country that it shares with the rest of the world. The balance between the doctrine and the factual issues show how much he was an ideologue in his reforms and how much he was an emerging public relations man who took his public's daily problems into account. His political profile emerged along with his bodysnatched language.

The problems he and his fellow communists faced were serious. He still had difficulty in letting go of the ideological lingo when he described the problematic issues and the U.S. role there. He enumerated them as "class struggle," "aggressive forces of imperialism," "nuclear hostages of the United States," "exploitation," "capitalism," "warmongers," "U.S. militarism," and "counterrevolutionary crusades." The rest of the problems (73.3%) was a consequence of this. It was "war and peace" and "aggravation of international tension."

Any communicator with a political purpose has to identify himself with something—if he is a communicator-at-home he is loyal on the surface to his ideology, its establishment, and its followers. He has, or at least he says he has, a program to improve or sustain social conditions or put an end to social ills. This program is expressed in the demands he makes. He realizes of course that there is or might be opposition to his program and ideology. This he takes care of by referring to his opposition whether the opposition is there for everyone to see, or as in a dictatorship, condemned to an underground existence. How he describes the opposition he faces is revealing of the strength of his power. It has been observed many times that the more derogatory the communicator is in his references to his adversaries, the more unsure he is of his position even though he may pay only slight attention to them in his message. In the United States, for instance, a desperate accusation—furlough for condemned murderers—in the 1988 Republican, early underdog campaign against the Democratic opposition is a case in point. In the 1996 presidential campaign the same technique was repeated in the desperate insinuations of lack of moral character against one of the candidates.

It also has been proved that the balance among the three categories any communicator uses in a political speech—identifications, demands, and opposition—reveals the communicator as a dictator or as a public relations specialist. In short, we get his psychological-political profile. In general, the dictator pays more attention to his ideology than to reforms, opposition, or the facts of an issue.

The public relations specialist is known for leaning more and more toward the patterns of balance in communications that have been used for a long time in Western democracies. That is, he tries to pay more attention to the facts of an issue, less attention to his ideology, and is more concerned with any opposition since his hallmark is sensitivity to his public's reactions and interests. This trend of communicating along Western patterns was already obvious in France in 1945 with the Socialist government, which was overwhelmed by its problems. The flight from ideology also sometimes spilled over among such diverse politicians as Salvador Allende and Fidel Castro, one more successful than the other (K. Dovring, 1975).

What profile does Gorbachev display in the first speech to his countrymen about Leninism? A public where Lenin's teaching is taken for granted and accepted? Gorbachev has been described as an expert in manipulating public opinion, and a great theatrical actor, a great persuader both at home and abroad, an expert in fitting his body language to his counterpart's mood, a genius in his ability to reach people on all levels, a man who could listen, and a man who could use both humor and anger to his own advantage (Sheehy, 1990).

In this talk to his countrymen, his attention is carefully balanced. His identifications cover over 46.7 percent of his message, his demands amount to 17.9 percent, and the opposition and problems he faces cover over 35.4 percent of his concepts. In 1918 and 1919 Lenin delivered one of his most important speeches with an identical balance (K. Dovring, 1965b). This not only shows how close he was to Lenin's attitude as a communicator, but also shows the similarity of their political situations: Revolution is around the corner, there are times of stress ahead. This balance in communication is shared by other revolutionaries, among them Martin Luther King Jr. in his letter from the jail in Birmingham, Alabama, in 1963, and a British economist, who in 1961 advocated a far-reaching revolution in agriculture and technology. We also meet here a very usual phenomenon: Differences in doctrines do not necessarily mean differences in attitudes to reach different goals. This may be a shocking and disagreeable discovery for most of us.

Then, we can ask if Gorbachev is an optimist or a pessimist and how powerful an image he wants to display to the world. The answer is still a matter of balance in his use of favorable or unfavorable concepts. No less than 82.8 percent of all his symbols in his talk emphasize the positive side of his power and strength. Only 17.2 percent recognize that there are some obstacles. This is an attitude that he shares with several powerful leaders. The balance in his communication is almost identical, for instance, with the Vatican's world-famous encyclical *Rerum Novarum* of 1891 which launched a new radical and social labor program in a troubled world of labor and unrest. All these social crises made it necessary for a powerful image to be attached to a reformer. Gorbachev's approach is also identical with the Vatican encyclical of 1941, which also had to emphasize its faith and power against all odds in a war torn world. Again we have to face the fact that different ideologies do not always create different attitudes in the communication of factual problems. No wonder that Gorbachev later established Soviet diplomatic representation in the Vatican.

Are there any undercurrents behind all this posturing of power and optimism? While his symbols of identification now are no less than 100 percent favorable when he expresses his political ego, and his demands for reforms are launched in a 100 percent positive attitude—the positive side of demands must always be emphasized when a communicator appeals to the public for his serious reforms—the problems and obstacles in his program are carefully balanced in his estimate of the opposition's strength. In that opposition, 51.3 percent are looked upon as manageable while no less than 48.7 percent is a headache. That is, he realizes that opposition to his reform is a powerful force that makes his chances of success not at all guaranteed. His balanced profile is, in fact, very close to Mao Tse-tung's speech in 1967 about the "Building of Our Country." That speech was delivered in a potentially revolutionary situation just as shaky as Gorbachev's own (K. Dovring, 1965b).

The public seldom has opportunity to see these balances—the analyst and the media people should. The *themes* his talk builds up are easier for the public to follow. Three categories become obvious to the naked eye. One is the *authority* who talks to the public. The other is *social issues* that are discussed. The third is the *negative problems*, among them the opponents, that the communicator condemns openly. References to this authority take up 31.4 percent of the concepts in his speech. It is described as "Soviet government and Lenin," "world socialism and Comrades," and "socialism means peace." His authoritative sponsors are also described as "the Soviet people and its armed forces," "Lenin's principles for peace," and "mankind's transition to socialism." It is the character of this authority that puts its heavy hand on the meaning of the words used in his message, sponsors the policy for the social issues, and colors the meaning of the solution of the social problems and world peace.

No less than 68.6 percent of his concepts discuss social issues such as "reasonable organization of international relations," "world security," "socialist states," "dictates of imperialism," "detente and nuclear war," "people's liberation," and "social and political progress." It is obvious that all these familiar words such as "international relations," "reasonable organization," "world security," and so on, as well as "social and political progress," must be closely observed as to their meaning because of their ideological contexts. "They don't use the words in the same meaning as we do," is still a valid observation of this Body-snatched English.

Then, among these 68.6 percent problems, 13.2 percent point to absolute obstacles to his program. Mostly he condemns them as "aggressive circles in the United States," "imperialism," "war party," "force," and "war propaganda." The balance here is similar to the socialist president Salvador Allende, whose speech to the United Nations in 1972 also was made in a time of efforts for deep-seated reforms.

Gorbachev is very much aware of the world listening in on his speeches to Soviet communists and other followers around the globe. He paints himself as a man deeply concerned with practical issues at home and abroad, but he does not leave his Leninist convictions behind. Meanwhile his talk is so balanced that he approaches the pattern of Western communications with its interest in the facts of an issue. On the other hand, he is still aware of the old ideological foe, the United States, and its "aggressive propaganda." He comforts his fellow communists with the assurance that Lenin's teachings will solve the problems even though, as we have seen from the balance of his themes, his authority is actually no more than one-third of the strength of the opposition when he confronts it.

It is in this loyalty to Leninism that all the familiar words of "peace," "disarmament," "security," and "economic relations on a democratic basis" should be interpreted. The balance in his use of concepts and themes makes the individual concept and individual word tainted. He is still very much a communicator-at-home.

In short, "peace and European security"; "elimination of hunger," "poverty," and "disease on earth"; "detente"; and "star wars"—all these problems—will be solved by a strong Soviet Union with a Leninist spirit. So, "peace is Socialism under Soviet leadership." This is the undercurrent beneath all the Western concepts and words in Gorbachev's speech. On the surface of the message, the balance is close to the French socialists of the postwar period in 1945 and to Khrushchev's party program of 1961. No wonder his public feels a new wind is blowing.

The tendency in his communication is close to that of a hardline Stalin communist, the prime minister and dictator of Bulgaria in the 1950s, the authoritarian Vatican of 1891, and also to Allende's speech of 1972. Allende was, as we recall, distrusted for his leftist leanings. The spectre of a dictator waiting in the wings was later confirmed by Gorbachev's longtime ally, the foreign minister Eduard Shevardnadze. This trend was also according to Lenin's philosophy. Many times Lenin repeated his opinion that the masses must be ruled for their own benefit. He believed they could not rule themselves.

It goes without saying that this Leninist socialist, Mikhail Gorbachev, who was out to change the world into "peaceful coexistence" was out for peace on his own terms and conditions. At least for now! Therefore, every essential concept in his speech must be interpreted according to his background and communist training, and according to the context in which the obvious ideological terms appear in his speech. Gorbachev is, however, not too sure about his success. The authority he exercised in this planned revolution at home and abroad covered, as we have mentioned, only 31.4 percent of his message. But the social and economic problems (55.4%) and the absolute negative foreign resistance that tried to prevent his reforms and take over the world (13.2%) amount together to no less than 68.6 percent of his two final themes. This meant not only a tough job ahead, but it also meant that he was in a weak position at home.

Public relations simply mean that in a realistic way the communicator takes into consideration not only the social problems that have to be discussed, but also people's minds, which cannot always be taken for granted. This is especially the case when reforms turn into revolution. That is in clear contrast to communication from a dictator in power who already concentrates on his ideological doctrine in his public messages, pays only token attention to reforms, and wholly neglects to mention any opposition or simply belittles it. It is in the undercurrents of a dictator's communication that his self-doubt or fear of an underground opposition comes to the fore.

On the other hand, the public relations–minded, more democratic communicator seems to give a very balanced and reasonable performance at first glance. Here, too, only the undercurrents of the words can indicate whether he is on his way to a dictatorship or if he will continue to balance his program and policy in a democratic way, consistent with what he displays for public consumption (K. Dovring, 1987; Lasswell, Leites, and Associates, 1949; Lasswell, Lerner, and Pool, 1952; Pool et al., 1951, 1952).

Lenin, like other dictators, did not have much confidence in the proletariat's ability to rule themselves. Someone must do it for them, he said many times. What is Gorbachev's opinion on this?

In December 1985 he again delivered a speech to the Soviet people. He called it "Creative Effort of the People. A Report to the All Union Scientific and Practical Conference in Moscow." From his book one can learn that the speech has been included because of "its significance." Did Gorbachev have any confidence in the proletariat?

As in his speech on Lenin's birthday, he still turns to his fellow communist countrymen with a sideglance to the followers abroad. He charms his Soviet audience by identifying them and himself in 37.3 percent of his concepts by reminding them of "our people and party, our scientists and the Soviet way of life." He emphasizes "human rights" and "socialism," "our peace-loving foreign policy," and dreams of "a world without weapon." "Economic expansion" is also noted while "information and vigorous propaganda" are set on a back burner.

The demands he makes—only 13.3 percent—admonish the people to "perseverance and complete dedication, to development of the Soviet people, and to constructive dialogue," but also to "political and ideological vigilance."

His worries take up no less than 49.4 percent of his attention. They are "global confrontation, American capitalists and monopolies who ensnare many developing countries." Then, the "United States is directly responsible for their starvation," the "United States' military aggression and neo-colonialism, the enemy is still the bourgeois society and imperialism" are added.

The balance of the concepts he identifies with (37.3%), what he demands (13.3%), and the problems that emerge (49.4%) clearly show that he is heading for trouble despite all his appeals and attention to the people's "creative efforts" and to the "ability of the Soviet people." No less than 70.5 percent of the problems are seen in a very dark light, a view that does not imply much confidence in the people's capacity—or his own—to solve the crises. Here Gorbachev is a man besieged by unmanageable problems and is only able to make a few hesitant demands to solve them. He is a troubled communicator with little confidence in his party and the people's efforts. In fact, the balance he uses in his concepts either applies to the surface of his message or to its undercurrents, or the themes his talk amounts to (the themes display no less than 63.1% problems, and of them, 34.8% impossible to solve, against 36.9% concepts of identifications devoted to socialism and the Soviet way of life as the solution). This sets him in the same powerless company not only with the fighting Lenin in his talks to the Russian people during the revolution 1918–19, but Gorbachev's approach is also the same as a beleagered communist collaborator and fellow traveler in Hungary in 1947. This was a time of stress and political insecurity in Hungary, and the fellow traveler had to talk officially on behalf of a coalition government and nonpartisan intellectuals to a world public about the need for economic reform in his country. At the time, the communists were only a fraction of the government coalition. The Hungarian collaborator dared not reveal his true identity, which he covered with his skillful double talk and Bodysnatched English.

It is this feature of doubt, both in the undercover communist in Hungary and now with Gorbachev, that Gorbachev's words take on a special meaning not necessarily obvious to a Western observer. His attacks, for instance, on those "who pose as champions for human rights" give the concept itself a problematic environment of "war, exploitation, subversion, propaganda and psychological warfare" while "Soviet military skill and loyalty to the Soviet Union" and "Soviet way of life" and "socialism" make up the authority for a "peace-loving foreign policy" that will enforce human rights. That is, the Western values in his talk get their meaning from the communist environment. It is a lingua franca international in appearance through the familiar words but parochial by its undercurrents, which results in bodysnatched language.

There is obviously something for everybody in his talk. The West can enjoy all the factual references to world problems and concern for world peace and developing countries as well as hope for a new attitude. Gorbachev's Soviet public can feel at home in the old aggressive concepts of "propaganda" and "exploitation" and "subversion" and "hypocritical champions of human rights" in the Western world. Meanwhile, Gorbachev himself carefully covers his authority as a ruler behind the "Soviet people." But as we have seen, this authority is not strong. His estimate of problems and opposition is always pessimistic, no matter the viewpoint from which one analyzes his message. That is, his belief in the "efforts of his people" to overcome all these troubles is not very strong. In fact, it seems to be nonexistent. Realism has taken over all wishful thinking along party lines while all thoughts of world development and peace are still captive in Soviet communist jargons and its ideas.

But Gorbachev has no longer confined his communication to

his home audience among communists. On December 18, 1984, he spoke in London to the British Parliament. This was a speech he also wanted to include in his book "because of its significance." Is his language and attitude here any different from his talk to his fellow communists?

Here he is abroad, both geographically and ideologically. Certainly, his appearance is a revolutionary event for the British and the world. So he starts to use his charm on his distinguished British audience. Obviously, he wants to appear as if he is in charge of the new situation. And he does. He identifies himself with the "wonderful British" by referring to the comradeship between Britain and the Soviet Union during World War II. But now both the British and the Soviets need to get more acquainted. Since 1970 Europe has been the cradle for the policy of *detente*. Political dialogue and cooperation between Western Europe and the Soviet Union is just as important for security as talk with the United States. "We have only one planet so we need constructive dialogue, scientific technological revolution, respect for security, international treaties," which are all concepts Gorbachev strongly identifies with as his own. This takes up 45.7 percent of his concepts, which makes him a communicator comparatively in control of the situation since the problems and demands together occupy just a bit more of his message, 54.3 percent.

This pattern of communication is again very close to the socialists in postwar France in 1945. The balance in the different categories of identifications, demands, and problems leads us back to Khrushchev's party program of 1961 and to Castro's First Declaration of Havana the same year. The political times and economic situations surrounding these speeches were similar in their social tensions and new economic beginnings.

At first glance, Gorbachev appears in his speech to the British to be a moderate, accommodating power holder. He seems to realize clearly that his 45.7 percent identifications do not master his 28.9 percent demands or challenge his 25.4 percent problems. His demands therefore appeal to "mutual understanding," "concrete steps to removing the threat of nuclear war," and that "we must coexist." The difficulty is that there is still danger of warfare, cold war, and nuclear threats. Not the least among the problems is the U.S. "dictation of its will to other nations." The "United States is the creator of mistrust and hostility by its old stereotypes."

In short, he tries to present himself to his audience as a master of the situation, but his power gets eroded by his demands and problems. Together these two categories cover 54.3 percent against his 45.7 percent identifications. He is not a strong leader, but he is very much aware of the serious situation. His communication approaches the models of Western democratic politicians. He is very much aware of his public and its needs: He has turned into a public relations man and salesman.

Nevertheless, if one asks how he uses his symbols, they are all cast in an optimistic vein. This 100 percent optimism despite all insecurity is a posture that he shares with many politicians on both the national and international scene, no matter what ideology they profess or deny they have. We can find it, for instance, with John F. Kennedy in the United States, with Khrushchev in the Soviet Union, with Eva Peron in Argentina, and with a host of others. This optimism functions as a smokescreen for the public when any politician wants to build up confidence in his program. If you don't behave as if you believe in your own program, nobody else will believe in it either. Gorbachev also wants to convince his public that he is on the right track.

This happy persuasion of the public dominates the undercurrents in all three categories of Gorbachev's message, whether he talks about values he identifies with, demands he makes for reforms, or the problems that may prevent him from saving the world. So on the surface it is a very rosy picture of a man in charge—not a dictator—who talks to the rest of the world and wants a respectful, peaceful dialogue with the "admirable" British. But he stresses that all this must happen under "Soviet leadership," since the "Soviet attitude at the negotiating table" is in "plain and unambiguous terms." However, this "leadership" tends to taint all the familiar, simple words of "peace" and "close cooperation" and "mutual understanding," as well as "peaceful dialogue" and "detente, security and equality." The meanings of the words have a new Soviet slant not found in the established English dictionaries, and this opens the way for Bodysnatched English.

But there are also a few literal traces of the old communist lingo used in front of the British audience. Khrushchev's "peaceful coexistence" is there just as is his "concrete form of cooperation." These expressions were first used by Khrushchev in his conference with Tito in Bucharest in August 1957 (Radio Moscow, August 1–2, 1957). Gorbachev also calls for "concrete steps and concrete moves" to "remove the threat of nuclear war." These steps should be followed by "correct" and "constructive dialogue." These communist symbols are more spectacular since they only take up 7 percent of his concepts. The other 93 percent concern political and social facts.

The topic of his speech to the British, the factual content that is more or less obvious to the public and may or may not coincide with the issues of the day and public interests, deals with two things: The social issue under debate and the authority that is necessary for solving the problems. No less than 73 percent of Gorbachev's talk concerns detente and nonproliferation of nuclear arms, political dialogue, Soviet-American agreement, intensification of trade, peaceful coexistence, and European frontiers.

Only 27 percent refer to the authority who is supposed to do something about all these issues. This authority is composed of Soviet leadership and includes British industrialists and businessmen plus "ties between our peoples." The public relation man courting his public has arrived on the global political scene.

In this final analysis there are no negative themes repulsive enough to be condemned. The balance here in his communication is close to Mao Tse-tung's in 1967 and the Rockefeller Panel Reports for "Prospect for America" in 1961. Their messages were also launched in times urgent for change and solution of national and international problems.

Gregory Bateson, the well-known philosopher, once said that without context there is no meaning. Applied to the research here, it is obvious that the meanings of the words in Gorbachev's talk are a matter of context (Bateson [1972], 1988). Context gives meaning to a word not only through a word's immediate environment in a text, but just as important, by the psychological and ideological attitude or profile of the speaker. That is why the balance in his use of words also creates the model of communication that makes a speaker a hardliner in his ideological

profile or a budding reformer who strives to free himself from
ideological ties when he advocates social and political issues.
That is why "Who says it?" or "Who are you?" are just as important questions as "What is said?"

In May 1985 Gorbachev played gracious host to two friends
of socialist leanings. One was, as we said, India's prime minister
at that time, Rajiv Gandhi. The other was Willy Brandt, president
of the Socialist International and leader of West Germany's Social Democratic Party. Here Gorbachev might be among political
friends but not necessarily faithful followers. So he still may be
a communicator-abroad despite the fact that the different occasions are an elegant lunch and a similar dinner in the Kremlin
for the two guests.

Gandhi, the first to arrive, came to dinner on May 21. Brandt
was a luncheon guest six days later. Let us first see how Gorbachev courts Gandhi, the representative of a sophisticated, old-
culture country with an open mind and often high achievements
in some areas of modern technology—a country that seriously
struggles to take its place among the technologically developed
nations.

In his dinner speech, Gorbachev tries to draw his guest's attention to the common character of the two "peace-loving
nations." These "comrades identifications" cover 61 percent of
his message. The demands he makes cover only 16.9 percent.
The problems he envisions amount to 22.1 percent—together
they create a challenge of 39 percent. This is a pattern of communication that presents Gorbachev as a man of power in command of his position. It is very close to the Vatican's labor
encyclical, the *Rerum Novarum* of 1891, and its no less famous
messages of 1931 and 1941. All these documents have one thing
in common—and as we have seen, it is not the first time Gorbachev communicates like the authoritarian Vatican—the messages are all delivered in times of strong tension and renewal by
rulers who want to emphasize their hold on power despite all
challenges to their authority. Gorbachev's identifications unite
everybody in the Soviet Union and India in their peace efforts
in the world. This is expressed by many polite welcome phrases.
It also emphasizes the Soviet's support for India's independence,
their common economic ties and joint space ventures, India's

"great people," and its acceptance of Stalin prizes. Last but not least, there is India's policy of nonalignment, which is India's contribution to world peace. His tone is upbeat: 88.9 percent of his concepts are handled in a positive way and only 11.1 percent permit some misgivings to appear. The tendency that carries his message, and that of many other communicators, is more a psychological factor than an ideological one. As we have pointed out before, a communicator who wants to succeed in his performance must wholly or mostly show optimism on the surface if his audience is to take him seriously. That explains why one can find the same optimistic tone not only with Gorbachev but also with most other rulers of government from early times to our days (K. Dovring, 1975).

The 16.9 percent demands Gorbachev makes are closely connected to the symbols he identifies with both himself and his guest, and they ask for "joint cooperation to end the arms race," "bilateral talks," "prevention of militarization of space," and "deepening of Soviet-India relations."

The opposition he faces against his reforms—22.1 percent of his concepts—are mostly caused by the United States and its influence in the Third World, U.S. imperialism and the arms race, and because of this, the greatly increased risk of nuclear war. The rest of the problems address, in general, terms about the risks to peace and security. Then, as an afterthought, come India's own major problems in development and also the general political power pressures in Asia. In short, peace and collaboration in Asia is the dream that the United States turned into a nightmare by its policy.

However, despite Gorbachev's optimistic performance when calling for his guest's attention and his need to throw a favorable light on the issues of the day, the undercurrents of his speech, as in that of many other communicators, tell the real story. Even when his identifications and demands are launched in a 100 percent optimistic vein, the problems come to a fore as rather difficult. It can go either way when he considers his ability to solve them; 50.5 percent describe them as unmanageable while 49.5 percent hope for the best. That is, his undercurrents amount to a declaration of distrust in solving the problems despite his calls for unity with India, which he has been so attentive to. This pattern is nothing new among political communicators. Distrust of the future is typical for many who on the surface appear to be in command. A closer look at their message, though, reveals their insecurity and pessimism in times of tension and stress. President Richard M. Nixon expressed similar distrust when he talked about school busing and his relations to the U.S. Congress (K. Dovring, 1975). And the revolutionary Lenin and his secret collaborator in Hungary in the 1950s, for example, were among the most pessimistic. But the line stretches from the Vatican of 1891 and the Stalinist communist in the Bulgarian government in the 1950s to messages from Kim Il Sung in North Korea to Qadhafi's *The Green Book* of 1976, as well as to Michael Dukakis, once a presidential candidate. Illustrations don't stop there. Both Jimmy Carter and Ronald Reagan showed undercurrents of deep pessimism in some of their messages, as did an immigrant to the United States, Nobel prize winning novelist Alexander Solzhenitsyn, who in an article in the *Washington Post* in 1978 showed a pessimistic undercurrent similar to Gorbachev's. Solzhenitsyn's strong pessimism influenced both his demands on the new world and the problems facing him despite his declaration of identification with his new life in a foreign part of the world. He later returned to his homeland.

Finally, what does Gorbachev serve his guest at the dinner? His menu offers three dishes: The *social issue*, the *authority* who may make decisions about it, and finally *problems* that are so odious that one can do nothing about them for the time being. These three categories are typical staples that any communicator may wind up with as the result of his performance.

The social issue dominates the table talk by no less than 48.6 percent. The emphasis is on political reality, so Gorbachev asks for the elimination of war, poverty, and disease and calls for work on lasting peace. This cannot happen without the help of an authority. References to this use up 40.3 percent of his message and make the authority at this point not quite so strong as the social challenges. The authority is built up by the collaboration between India and the Soviet Union with the help of the People's Republic of China and members of nonaligned nations. But whatever strength the authority has is further undermined by 11.1 percent negative references to the United States, its arms race and military superiority, and its insistence on star wars. This is in addition to its "spheres of vital interest" and its "military blocs and profit makers." Together with the social challenges he already mentioned, these additional problems obviously dim Gorbachev's chances for success. His 40.3 percent authoritative power is suddenly faced with all together 59.7 percent problematic questions about world stability. The only communicator on record who has displayed an identical profile was the hard-core Stalinist, Bulgarian prime minister Vulko Chervenkov, who in 1950 tried to communicate his strength and power to his people while his references to his country's social troubles already in his undercurrents revealed him as a colossus on clay feet.

Gorbachev insists that his whole message to India is a call for peace on earth. This effort should be led by the Soviet Union, but it does not trust that India and other nations are not going to be swallowed up by the "profit-hungry," "militaristic United States" in the process. That is, here the Soviet Union itself is a political colossus on clay feet despite its benevolent struggle for peace. Gorbachev's "peace" comes out as a *Pax Sovietica* in his Bodysnatched English and taints all his "peaceful collaboration" and similar concepts with communist meanings. This trans-English is further emphasized when he describes the United States as the main obstacle to world peace in terms that harken back to the cold war's jargon. Factual, practical issues such as nuclear power, security, poverty, sickness, and so on all have the tone of Soviet Union as the Big Brother. But to the public, who mostly observes the familiar words that describe mutual problems, the speech is an act of public relations by a seemingly powerful political figure who is seriously concerned with their well-being now and in the future. But wasn't this dinner speech aimed at a fellow ruler and his aides? Yes, it was, but one must always remember nowadays that what is said at a special occasion can immediately show up in the public domain through the media. In our time there is no privacy in communication, especially not on the political scene.

The luncheon for Willy Brandt a week later in the Kremlin was another opportunity for Gorbachev to make his opinion known to a potential ally and to get an exercise in the new emerging public relations. Here Gorbachev shares a model of

communication with many other politicians of different persuasions who were facing a new time and serious challenges to their
old politics. Among them was Fidel Castro in his "First Declaration of Havana," as well as Pope John XXIII in 1961 and his
successor, Paul VI, in their messages from the Vatican. In 1967,
Mao Tse-tung added to the same pattern when he talked about
"Building Our Country." All these leaders wanted to draw the
public's attention to their surface identifications, demands, and
problems.

Always the polite host, Gorbachev here is no exception and
greets his guest, Willy Brandt, by drawing his attention to their
common identifications of socialism and its various forms, as
well as common demands and common problems. This is one
way to make a guest feel at home. His identifications are
strong—55.9 percent of his message—and overwhelm both his
demands and problems. Most of his identifications are greetings
that emphasize "constructive talks" that will create "truly neigh-
borly relations and productive cooperations between European
capitalist and socialist countries." Next he stresses "East-West
peace by the elimination of nuclear weapons and star wars." He
respects "the world community and the strength of European
security, the mood of the masses and mankind." Clearly, the
public relations man, opening his arms to his public and its
needs, is very much in evidence.

His demands, 20.9 percent of his talk, call for "exploration of
outer space for peaceful purposes—a mutual endeavor—for reduction of the arms race and for complete elimination of nuclear
weapons." He also wants "security for the European continent,
normal relations among good neighbors, a new international
economic order, overcoming of backwardness," and finally a
"firm political will for peace."

The obstacles to this program are evaluated in his 23.2 percent
problems. They are "arms race and reactionary forces, the United
States' plans to militarize space, star wars and the fact that Hitler's fascists have not learnt their lesson from the past." "The
escalation of nuclear weapons" is also on his mind. And then,
of course, there are "the problems of relations among developing
countries and the very real threat of hunger, disease, illiteracy,
colonial past, industrial capitalist countries, and the issue of de-

veloping countries' independence." Still he wants to show Willy Brandt that Gorbachev is in control despite the fact that demands and unsolved problems cover together 44.1 percent of his speech while the references to his own power are a meager 55.9 percent. But this is hardly a dictator's approach. It looks more like a seemingly reasonable powerbroker's display of reality, or at least an open mind to reality.

Gorbachev displays the same show of strength and control of the situation in the way he uses all his concepts. No less than 81.1 percent are dealt with in a favorable vein, while only 18.9 percent show a darker side. He uses here the same highhanded approach as other rulers in power, both among social reformers of the Vatican and among socialists such as Chile's Allende. We can remember here, as before, that a communicator who wants his public to believe in him and his program must present it in an optimistic mood if he wants to evoke confidence with the public.

However, there is a sinister picture developing when one looks at the undercurrents of his talk. Even though concepts he identifies with and his demands are 100 percent positively described, the truth comes out when he refers to his problems. No less than 81.7 percent of them are described as unmanageable, while only 18.3 percent have a chance of being overcome. This dark pessimism creates a model of communication that is not found among his totalitarian predecessors in the Soviet Union or in other nations. It is a sign of his realism despite his surface optimism. It is also an opening for modern public relations to enter where a public who can see for itself the problems of the everyday world is considered. This is today's public, who all over the world, has started to question authority and wants the communicator to recognize the problems for what they are and to be included in his future plans.

One would expect that such realism would be carried over when he talks about the *practical issues* and the *authority* who wants to take care of them. Of his themes 34.5 percent point to this authority, which is composed of the Soviet Union, the communists, and the Social Democratic Party of Germany, which "stands for progress." Already the issues in need of solutions cover no less than 65.5 percent of his talk. Among them are 46.6

percent referring to "detente, space problems, normal relations, equal international relations, new economic international order, constructive co-operation, peace and security, interests of the people." The rest, 18.9 percent, are leftovers from the cold war and still threaten by evoking current troubles such as "arms race, reactionary forces, United States' plans to militarize outer space, danger of war and truly global destruction, chemical weapons and nuclear war."

The pattern of communication of his themes still shows the same balance used by the Vatican's religious-political-social encyclical of 1891 on labor relations, as well as by Allende in his themes of 1972. All three of these documents were released in times of a new politically and socially changing world.

Both Gorbachev and his predecessors in communication have had their authority overwhelmed by the problems that face them: the authority Gorbachev claims he has—34.1 percent—is no match for the reality that is closing in on him. No less than 65.9 percent describe the problematic issues he has to solve in order to succeed. That is, his is a weak position of power and he knows it, even though one has to dig into the undercurrents of his speech to see what is behind the face he shows to his West German guest, whose cooperation he desires so strongly. As he said himself once: I am no simpleton.

What does this balance do to his trans-English or Body-snatched language? More than ever, his symbols refer to familiar words seemingly without any ideological bent. Rarely do words from the old ideological communist lingo creep in. But all the commendable words, such as peace and security, cooperation, and a Europe with nuclear-free zones, are diminished by his lack of power. The Leninist has been forced to go underground, and his words seem to be empty and cover more wishes than reality. In fact, his communication mirrors the political chaos that was waiting around the corner and challenged the Leninist in Gorbachev to publicly leave the communist party to its sinister fate. He again became a public relations man, this time because of his lack of dictatorial power before the overwhelming problems. In other words, he became a salesman hoping today's public would buy the goods he puts up for sale. But he also became a truly democratic communicator in the Western sense.

Outside the totalitarian communicators' circle, there exist only political and commercial power brokers, public relations experts, and salesmen who have to rely on the approval or disapproval of the public when they discuss an issue. The U.S. Congress is a case in point. This means that the democratic power is relative, negotiable, exposed, and changed according to the public's will and whims. Only a dictator can rely on his own power to bend the people's will with his politics and communications. All this is not only mirrored in the public opinion's rise against authority today, but consequently, it is also reflected in the speeches of political figures, in their choice of words, in the balance in the use of their words, in the kinds of interest (and lack of interest) in the topics their message eventually displays, and above all in the undercurrents of meanings of their words that by repetition and contexts create the bodysnatched language that can mislead or inform us all. As a public we should be aware, or to put it in the lingua franca of centuries ago: *Caveat emptor.*

8

Epilogue or Prologue?

Not long ago there was a writer in the former Soviet Union who devoted much of his time to studies of English. Eventually he became fluent in its use. When he later settled in the United States, he discovered to his surprise that all his reading of English in Russia had not at all prepared him to understand American life and the "inner working" of its society. He discovered that his command of idiom and nuance in English could never substitute for a "native mind-set" (Gurevich, 1991).

The power of communication realms and communicator-at-home or abroad cannot be more clearly expressed.

The difficulty involved in an individual freeing herself or himself from the power of their own communication realm and finding a clear vision of the character of other realms is commented upon by another writer (Krippner, 1980). He warned his readers that we all are not generally conscious of the effects of suggestive influences (he calls them brainwashing) that are all around us in our own communication realm. He emphasized how important it was for us as individuals and as members of our community to be aware of these influences from our education, not the least from media such as television, radio, cinema, music, environment, and so on. If we are not to become "victims" of our own culture any longer, we should be aware of these "suggestions of influence."

We can add to this that our time's global conversations in any media, at home and abroad, cry for awareness by the public if our world is to develop into a democratic society where leaders should be in continuous dialogue with their public in considering people's needs and desires.

"Interdependence among nations," the slogan of our time—illustrated so forcefully on the Internet—gets its strongest effect in communications. This happens regardless of the nation or ideological homeport the communicator claims in his artistic act, in his choice of words, concepts, and their meanings and the political and social attitudes this creates. Awareness of this performance eventually contributes to a critical observation of ourselves and other nations, and in the long run may thankfully limit international relations to peaceful conversations on any issue. So let us go eavesdropping and "let us reason" in our global village, and never take anything for granted. That is another kind of public uprising against limitless authority.

Appendix I

Shadows on the Political Screen: Undercurrents in Presidential Speeches from FDR to Bill Clinton

How do the leaders of the United States cope in their performance on the Superhighway of Communication? Whether they want it or not, they have to face a global public, be it at home or abroad. It is in this communication that social and political undercurrents of meaning play a greater role than ever. The clash of different cultures and political goals sees to this.

Franklin D. Roosevelt's political mentor, Louis Howe, said that "it is the undercurrents of politics that are difficult, sometimes impossible to cope with. When your opposition surfaces and you can see it, then you can respond to it." He was right, especially when it comes to political communication. But now we have an analysis that tries to reveal who and what this covert opposition is. It gives us its character and its undercurrents. We can also see how the communicator himself looks at this underground opposition and what his real interest is, no matter what he says in public, since on the surface any successful communicator must mirror his public's character and concerns.

My basis for this research has been Harold Lasswell's configurative analysis, developed further in intensive and thorough

Speech at the Policy Sciences Annual Institute, Yale Law School, New Haven, Connecticut, October 22–24, 1993.

recording of a message's quantitative and qualitative semantics, context of the words and concepts, and in the observation of the age and culture in which the message was delivered. I will give a few examples from this research of many years.

There is no lack of opportunity for such research today. The problem is growing more and more complicated since the United States has become the lonely superpower and its English is the globe's lingua franca. The ideological jargons are disappearing more and more, and there is a universal English that is very plain on the surface and used by many people the world over.

Then, we have today's electronic marvels of communication, but we still use and abuse them by methods as old as mankind. The power of the United States makes the American president's voice heard all over the world, whether he or she wants it to be or not. Domestic issues easily turn into international problems with a world that wants change but on its own terms. The plain English that is used illustrates this in its double talk. Familiar words and concepts receive bodysnatched meanings and can create undercurrents in all communications. When a presidential candidate comes home from a meeting with the Viet Cong and recommends "correct peace," look out!

Then, our contacts are not made easier by the fact that what we don't have in common, we cannot communicate. All these double and even triple meanings have practical effects on words and concepts not only in the media but also in summit meetings and other conferences. As previously mentioned, Kennedy had a bitter experience with this when he tried to talk with Khrushchev. Some have suggested that international political conferences should be carried out by multilingual politicians who could speak each other's languages. From the public's view, this is dangerous. The use of a common lingua franca, such as English, in conferences is a safeguard for the public who has a chance to follow what is going on behind the official supposed "frank discussion" statements (while the disclosures often depend on leaks or slips of the tongue).

We should not underestimate rhetoric then. It is the call for action or nonaction in our political and legal life. It is the preparation of the public for events to come (or not to come) and the opportunity, for instance, for a lawyer to tell a jury or his client of a problem's place in the community values.

As I said, we are traditionalists when we communicate despite our modern media. So let us pay a short visit to France during the French Revolution. The world was in turmoil when it came to languages as well. There were heated debates on what language—French, Russian, or British English—was most fit for universal use as a means of peace and for breaking down national barriers. Those who pointed out that a universal language did not mean peace because people were different and meant different things when they used the same words were ignored. This did not prevent the famous writer Jeanne Roland and her husband, who was powerful in the Girondist government, from writing an important essay—before the guillotine stopped them. They wrote in English and urged their countrymen to establish close relations, not only with Britain but above all—and this was the first time this was said—with the young republic across the Atlantic, the United States of America. Why? The Rolands were convinced that the United States was to be a great power in the future because of the advantages of its laws, its traditions, and its commerce. This American future influence was bound to spread all over the world, they wrote. To learn American English was a practical necessity. Talk about forecasts and prophecy!!!

Well, the world is learning American English, sort of, and the United States seems to have lived up to the Rolands' prophecy whether it wants to or not. This country has a unique position, not only in the world but also in its freedom to communicate. Our presidents have been free to choose from the old traditions of communication and pick whatever pattern is most efficient for the occasion. But there is no guarantee that the democratic pattern of communication—let us go to the people and tell them the facts—makes people responsive. We as a public are not specialists on all topics, such as taxation and all its ramifications. Bare facts never speak for themselves, not even in the telephone book. A mere name tells you nothing unless you know the person or unless the Yellow Pages tell you the name's significance in the community's values. A political communicator cannot reach the public without handling both facts and values. It is here that propaganda, bias, and distortion of facts get a real chance to come in.

What kinds of communication can a president pick that people are used to? There are, for instance, the official voices from the Vatican who, according to its encyclicals, have the duty to interfere in any social issues that have moral side effects. If we use Lasswell's configurative analysis, we see that the Vatican's public profile is very authoritative. Its attention is concentrated on its ideological values as expressed in colorful clerical vocabulary. This takes up the communicator's attention span at the expense of demands for social programs on labor relations, for instance, if this is the topic they claim to discuss. The opposition is often ignored or paid very little attention. The public gets an image of power in command, but in the undercurrents, the surface image is often shadowed by the rejection of the opposition, which was so neglected in the public profile. The undercurrents also reveal that the speaker's great interest is not labor relations, but the Vatican's own power. The real character of the opposition is not related to facts on labor relations, but to sinister opponents who threaten the Vatican's power over these relations. The profile may be softening under serious crises such as the fascists' attack on the Vatican in 1930 and during World War II, but the original pattern comes back as soon as the crises are past. The influence of Catholic doctrines among governments is world wide even though Evita Peron turned the tables and used both the pattern and the gesture of papal blessing for her own self-styled goddess image.

Inspired by the pattern and just as totalitarian in communications are the communists and fascists, as already noted by the author of *1984*, George Orwell. This shocks many who refuse to believe that different ideologies may use the same communication pattern. The colorful ideological vocabularies are used so frequently that Lasswell could, in times of war and crises, identify different persuasions by their special jargons.

All powers have their missionaries and revolutionaries. One was Lenin who, on unsteady feet, tried out his first attempts at revolution. His public attention was almost equally divided between his political ego and his opposition. There was almost no place for his revolutionary demands. Over 80 percent of his undercurrents further emphasized his real interest: the imperialists and capitalists who made all of Russia their victim.

Another revolutionary—in power—is Libya's Qadhafi. His *Green Book* reveals him as a colossus on clay feet. His undercurrents clearly reveal his self-doubts, and his view of all political systems in the world as the real opposition is, in his mind, cause enough to attack everybody, even by terrorist means.

As I said, ideologically revealing lingo is on its way out. Worldwide economic crises contribute to this just as much as the electronic global media. Ordinary English words are used everywhere and cover very different persuasions. Kennedy's language did not differ much from Salvador Allende's. People's Republic of China tries hard to cover up its undercurrents. Lately Gorbachev and Yeltsin are throwing off their communist chains. The new bland English as lingua franca nevertheless became the horror of the old diehard extremists who couldn't dream that the old ideologies might be alive and well under a lingua franca.

What should have appeared was a growing concern for understanding the meaning of this universal language's undercurrents and its use of familiar words and concepts for political purposes. It was in this understanding and disclosure that one could get the opportunity to respond to the real opposition; which Roosevelt's political mentor found almost impossible to face if it did not come out in broad daylight. Kennedy was not the only one to learn that these undercurrents changed familiar words in meaning and purpose.

It is not enough to list the ordinary words and their new meanings; one should also get a clear picture of the message by looking at the political character of the speaker or negotiator since, as we said, a political communicator succeeds by reflecting his public's attitudes—on the surface—while he instills in them his own purpose.

So, we have to know how he balances his values when he says that he talks about a fact. This balance reveals his undercurrents and how he identifies his real opposition. Eventually this uncovers his real purpose, his strength, and his weakness.

An American president, usually free from ideological straitjackets, can use any old pattern of communication he or she feels is appropriate for the occasion. Lyndon Johnson was pontifical even in his undercurrents when he tried to sell the Atlantic Alliance to the American people. Not even his apparent fear of nuclear war could unsettle his patronizing attitude, but this did not make him a dictator, only a true believer in America's might. He could not dictate in open societies.

Richard M. Nixon battled with ideological chains and prejudice in his talk about "school busing," once merely a word for transportation. It became bodysnatched as a term in education. Nixon tried to appear neutral to the public. His attention to the topic is equally divided between his authority to enforce the measure and to deal with its opposition. His mood is divided between optimism and pessimism.

His undercurrents tell another story. With the neutrality gone, school busing took on a highly negative association; but opposition against busing gave hope for the future. The real evil he found among the federal courts and the Congress, who insisted on school busing.

Meanwhile, Nixon was faced with problems of foreign policy on his very doorstep. In September 1972, North Korea's Kim Il Sung used America's open society to lay down the law in the *Washington Post*. Not quite with it, he still used communist lingo in his attempt at persuading America about his friendliness. His pattern of communication was reminiscent of Khrushchev's when Khrushchev opened up to the West. But Kim Il Sung's undercurrents revealed his doubts that he would be able to convince America that North Korea was just a victim of the Nixon doctrine and American imperialism.

Kennedy's inauguration speech and Gerald Ford's worries about the nation's economy are almost identical in their public profile. As one could expect from the occasion, Kennedy's speech was all expectations and optimism. Strangely enough Ford is just as optimistic about the country's economic trouble, but his undercurrents showed him as a weak power overwhelmed by unemployment and inflation, which he did not expect to master.

Another place where a politician's profile comes to public attention is in a presidential candidate's nomination acceptance speech. In 1988 George Bush paid close attention to his authority and the values he stood for—he was, after all, vice president then. He was already cast as a winner in an authoritarian sense—

his calls for social programs and his concerns with any opposition are slight.

Michael Dukakis, his competitor, paid less attention to his political identity than did Bush, but Dukakis was eager for social reforms. He was used to governing, where much opposition is overruled. In fact, he paid even less attention to opposition than Bush did. Both were in an optimistic mood, and took on the attitude that if you don't believe in your own program, nobody else will. Bush, however, was more optimistic than Dukakis. Bush's undercurrents reflected this in that even slight opposition received a gentle pat on the head. Dukakis suddenly was 100 percent positive in his undercurrents in referring to himself and his demands. But his optimism crumbled when he considered his opposition's character—it was 100 percent evil and diminished his authority for creating social progress. This was a lack of belief in himself and his social vision. Social issues were very much in his interest, but many of them were looked upon as impossible to solve. His authority to handle them was very weak, but this is not so unusual for a candidate for office. The problem was that Dukakis had a competitor who thought highly of himself. Bush's interest in social issues did not appear much in his undercurrents, where his political ego and authority occupied almost 90 percent of his interest. There he mirrored Ronald Reagan's second inauguration speech, in 1984, which devoted almost 80 percent to Reagan's political self at the expense of any interest in the many unsolved social issues still looming after his four years as president.

Bill Clinton's acceptance speech in July 1992 shows a public profile strong enough to reveal his confidence in his political ego and program. At this stage his demands for reforms were stronger than his attention to himself. The opposition he counted upon made no inroads in his authority. Publicly, he is optimistic, but not 100 percent. In his undercurrents we meet a candidate who is wholly confident in his political values and ego. When he demands reforms, he displays the same confidence, even though he does not underestimate his opposition.

If we then ask what Clinton is really interested in, he once more shows the same face as his public face—a rare event among politicians. But now the social problems weigh even heavier on his mind. Some of them are looming disasters, such as the millions of unemployed people, not to speak about the incumbent president, another disaster.

Clinton's inaugural address in January 1993 was close to the balance in values which Kennedy had used thirty years earlier. They show the same attention to political ego and to demands for social reforms without neglecting the problems. But they are not identical. Kennedy was more optimistic than Clinton. Clinton's undercurrents are 100 percent favorable when he refers to his political identity and demands for reforms—just as Reagan in 1984 and Dukakis in 1988. Like them, his look at the problems ahead is just as negative. All of them may have learned something as governors! But the similarity disappears when we remember that Reagan's interest in his political ego dominated his interest in social problems by 80 percent.

Clinton's interest, according to the undercurrents in his inauguration talk in 1993, creates a new political profile that I have not met before during my analyses. Almost 82 percent of Clinton's real interest covers social issues, none of them looked upon as impossible obstacles. His small interest in his personal authority grows even less self-centered when he claims that his authority comes from the "founding fathers" and the American people. He is obviously a social reformer who expects to fight together with his fellow citizens against his opposition, an issue revealed as increasing economic inequality in the country.

The only other document I have analyzed that comes close to this overwhelming interest in social issues is the scholarly Rockefeller Report of 1951, written by a committee of 100 citizens and published as *Prospect for America*. It remained an academic exercise in revolution.

A few words about body language. Our world has gone from the clenched fist—which you can still find in Somalia—to the greeting from those who wanted to transform the world into a military camp—Heil Hitler!—and from the single V-sign "for Victory" used by Churchill but later narrowed by Nixon into two V-signs wrapped around himself (cf. Desmond Morris, 1994).

Clinton has widened the single V-sign into two open, outstretched arms, embracing victory to be shared by everybody.

He used this gesture when he gave his inauguration speech. This same gesture embraced the leaders of the PLO and Israel in the White House rose garden. And we can often see that he uses the same gesture on television if we need more proof. Obviously, he invites us all to come!

Appendix II

Tracing Undercurrents in English as Lingua Franca: From Ronald Reagan to Moammar Qadhafi

We face two worlds in conflict when we analyze yesterday's and today's communications from what has been called the "political people"—that is, the politicians and their handlers—when they grasp for power over minds and decisions. This conflict is bound to happen. One world that tries to get its voice through the political communications is the scholars, the learned specialists who deliver carefully researched facts for our information. Their vision must necessarily be limited by the character of the scientific facts. The other world that tries to overpower the scholars is the domain of the creative, political artists—the political actresses and actors. They borrow from the same scholarly facts to serve *their* vision of the reality and purpose that they force or invite the public to share, depending on the society's character of dictatorship or democracy. The public opinion researchers then take over with their polls and record the public reaction: blind obedience on the surface in a dictatorship, mixed quality of answers in a democracy.

The communication process is an act of attention, interest, influence, and understanding. Unless a communicator is a specialist on a certain topic and the audience shares his or her interest, all communicators must start their contact with the public with appeals to the public's attention to their community values. The general public cannot be knowledgeable about all topics and facts, but community values are well known to them from their early education. These values are the key to their attention. Key symbols or community values always have a positive or negative undercurrent stemming from the official ideology of a community, such as human rights or murder. It is in this light that the communicator offers his facts of a topic to the mass public. If it serves his purpose it is here he is tempted—more often than not—to abandon the limitations of scholarly facts and become a creative artist who paints the facts according to his own vision of them. There the real intention of his message is revealed by the undercurrents this process creates. The more community values he uses, the less attention he pays to the character of the facts themselves. This influences the quality and the themes of his message. The public's attention span is usually short, especially short in times of war and other crises when fast action is needed. So, community values crowd his message, are repeated *ad nausean,* and eventually overwhelm it, and a special vocabulary emerges. This continuous repetition of a community value is the base of all propaganda—and learning!

The results are many through the ages: We face communist jargons, fascist terms, religious fanatics and their lingo, and so on. All these jargons were areas for research during times of war as well as in other critical periods. Their appearance was recorded and their influence noticed among the public, and caused special legislation. In short, the public attention span became a fruitful field for research on allies' and enemies' plans and movements during wars. Later, in times of peace, scholars dreamed of and carried out world attention surveys of community values whose presence or absence signaled whether the world was planning a war or working for peace or just negotiations. The world became accustomed to the colorful jargons that clearly indicated who was talking.

But something happened. Electronic media started to spread over the world on a scale never before experienced by mankind. The media's reach opened political and national borders believed closed forever. Political jargons started to disappear or vanished all together. Much of the world was listening in and simple talk that would be understood was needed. American English was always used by the media in this global contact—sometimes reluctantly. English was English was English, and it became the world's lingua franca. It was assumed that everybody could understand everybody no matter what delicate problems were discussed. We had dictionaries, didn't we? So, peace would be the result of our communications. But it soon became very clear that English was used in a new way by different nations and interests when they talked. It was necessary to question who the communicator was, about his ideological and cultural background, about his professed political goal, and about his native language. And what did he say that he identified with, what were his demands, which problems did he have to tackle? This was the jungle to get through before one could address the substantial facts he claimed to talk about. Here the scholars and scientists at last got a chance to be useful (unless the analysts already knew all this background information themselves). But this was far from influencing the communicator himself.

When the communicator started to use less jargon or did not use it at all, he seemed more familiar to those with English as their mother tongue. But a closer analysis of the communicator's speech gave another view of the goals and purpose and attitude to problems he discussed than was given by his English words. This also influenced the speaking habits of those who had English as their mother tongue because communication is a two-way street. Ordinary English words acquired meanings different from established use. For instance, ideologies were declared dead by optimists around the world. But not quite. For example, a basic theme in Lenin's teachings was his belief in the *correctness* of his policy. "Correct policy" was a high frequency concept in his followers' speeches and could be found anywhere among faithful communists in various nations. But the idea of correct policy did not stop there. "Correct solution to peace" was recommended by a U.S. senator to his American home public when he returned from a conference with the Viet Cong. Today, the concept of correct policy is incorporated into all kinds of social conditions—sometimes jokingly, sometimes very earnestly—in the United States. The fact is that the concept is an example of lingua franca that did not at all belong in a Western democracy where no policy is "absolutely correct;" democracy in the West is a matter of diversity and compromise. The undercurrent in the concept of correctness is of absolute truth and dictatorship and obedience that has wormed its way into the United States by lingua franca and given us another illustration of the success of undercurrents.

Then there is the example of the Swedish concept of "ombudsman" now found everywhere in the United States. Ombudsman in Sweden, a community value there, is a watchdog for the legislature against the judiciary and the administration, and is an independent force. In the United States ombudsman lost its Swedish undercurrent and became taken over by the American undercurrent of corporate culture and became a sounding board for grievances within the same firm. This means that lingua franca is a give and take—not necessarily good, not necessarily bad—but it is an important feature in global communications both at home and abroad.

Let us take a look at two different communicators who, because of their powerful positions, have had to talk to and be listened to by the whole world even though their targets include their home communities. One has English as mother tongue, the other uses English as lingua franca. Both of them are still of consequence today and try to influence the world. One is Ronald Reagan, fortieth president of the United States, and still a living political influence as demonstrated by the acceptance of his economic policies by the Republican party. The other one, not quite so accepted and called the "pariah of the World" by the media, is Moammar Qadhafi, ruler over the oil-rich country of Libya and also suspected as a terrorist.

The occasion for the Reagan speech we study here is the acceptance speech of his nomination for four more years as president of the United States. The date was August 1982. In 1,039 concepts he declares his willingness to accept the nomination. The special colorful jargon is missing, and he uses a familiar choice of words. He has a reputation of being a great communicator, as an actor he was a professional performer on both the artistic and political scene. On the surface his pattern of speaking follows other democratic speakers. In the distribution of his identifications, demands, and problems, 47.5 percent are devoted to what symbols he identifies with, and his demands take up 19.4

percent. Remarkable, however, is that the problems he faces cover no less than 33.1 percent of his attention—this after four years in office with supposedly rich opportunities to solve the problems. Obviously, he wants to direct the public's attention to the fact that he has not exercised any effective power. Burdened with a Congress in which the House was democratic and only the Senate at that time was republican, he hopes for more power in times to come. His pattern of communication is close to that of a dreamer in Great Britain who hoped for an agricultural revolution but was not sure of the outcome (K. Dovring, 1965b). This tendency to dream of new beginnings comes clearly to the fore when we look at the distribution of the favorable and unfavorable light over the concepts. Positive themes take up 66.9 percent of his message, while negative themes cover 33.1 percent. This is a state of mind that is very close to that of the French socialist government immediately after World War II, when France was in economic distress and its government called for a new beginning.

As we said, the attention a communicator pays to community values and facts in his message is not the whole story. But community values in English are an important introduction to those who use English as lingua franca. Then we ask what kind of attention he gives the values and facts in his speech and the distribution of favorable and unfavorable light on his identifications, demands, and problems. At this time we meet not only the community values and facts but what he means by using them and how. We meet the undercurrents in his talk. His speech has seven themes and in five of them he identifies himself in a positive way. The first—"our administration"—turns out to be the president and his party, a not surprising undercurrent. 46.7 percent of the identification symbols there are positive, and only 8.4 percent demand some improvements—on all seven topics his demands are described in a positive way. But there is another story when he describes his problems. On all seven topics his problems are described in a negative way as an obstacle to his programs, and his topic of "our administration" is no exception. The problems his administration faces are no less than 44.9 percent of resistance. This is indeed a weak power position. The next topic he talks about is "the American dream," which is given undercurrents of "our liberties" and "our values." The identifications are 72.5 percent favorable here, the demands are few, only 8.1 percent, and the problems are a mere 19.4 percent. His patriotism is strong.

The next issue discusses "our Allies." His attention to them is positive on the surface; he identifies with 35.1 percent of the symbols on the topic, his demands cover only 6.1 percent. But then the mirror shatters since no less than 58.8 percent of the topic create problems. Together with the 6.1 percent demands on the allies, the problems concern no less than 64.9 percent of our relations. That is, the allies are a pain in the neck according to the undercurrents here.

After this, Reagan turns to his faith in our Lord, a favorable topic that occupies 38.2 percent of his thoughts. The undercurrents here show that the concept of our Lord is identical with "one nation under God" and "parochial schools." The demands he makes on the topic are overwhelming—61.8 percent and mostly limited to demands for parochial schools as the most practical solution for divine dominance.

Despite the make-up of Congress—the next topic—Reagan looks upon it in a positive way with 26.7 percent identifications. However, his undercurrents on the topic identify him only with that part of the Congress where the Senate is in control, and the House can be tolerated only by the help of "concerned Democrats in the House." So the community symbol of the Congress has the undercurrent of a republican Congress and a few enlightened House democrats—which of course will be confusing to those who use lingua franca and interpret the community symbol, the Congress, as an American unity. Then, his demands on the topic take up the rest of his attention, 73.3 percent, but ignore any problems.

At last, there are two topics he looks upon in such a negative way that he cannot identify himself with any of them. "nuclear war" is one. It has the terrible undercurrent of "doomsday weapons." To solve the problem, his demands take up no less than 77.3 percent of the discussion. The problems are evaluated in 22.7 percent of the concepts. Interesting is that the other negative topic in his message, "federal spending is out of control," has almost the same character as the ominous nuclear war in Reagan's mind. There are no identifications with the federal waste, but the demands for a remedy are almost of the same strength as those on nuclear war—77.2 percent. The problems on the topic are also close—22.8 percent.

On the surface of the message, "the attention span," Reagan talks about his administration, the American dream, our allies, our Lord, and the U.S. Congress while he condemns nuclear war and federal spending. The attentive public will get that message, but the undercurrents in his talk introduce to these community symbols partisan qualifications in meaning. It is up to the public opinion polls to discover their influence. The influence can be immediate or arise later. As we pointed out, this makes the meaning of the community symbols more difficult to handle in a lingua franca.

If we now look at the result of the analysis of Reagan's identifications, demands, and problems we have found that his identifications are always positive and so are his demands. But all his problems are described in a totally negative way. This means that the balanced pattern of communication we got from the categories on the surface and to which he drew the mass public's attention (47.5% identifications, 19.4% demands, and 33.1% problems) aren't supported by the undercurrents in his message. The undercurrents don't only give qualified meanings or partisan twists to well-known community symbols, but they also give another pattern of communication than what appears on the surface. Here his symbols of identifications and demands are 100 percent favorably addressed, and all the problems are 100 percent negative. This is a black and white picture of reality found in most primitive propaganda messages. Another interesting feature is noted if we compare his talk with a message from the New Far Left from the United States in the 1970s (K. Dovring, 1975). There the Far Left writer also offers identifications—but with a foreign power by symbols 100 percent positive—and the demands are 6.8 percent favorable and 93.2 percent negative since the communicator does not believe that he will ever see them met. And all the problems he considers are looked upon in 100 percent negative light. So, what we have here from Rea-

gan's message is close to the Far Left's communication in reverse—that is, we have encountered the program of the New Far
Right.

Finally, what are the themes that emerge from his message?
What is he interested in? His message creates three themes, but
they don't concentrate on facts. One is concerned with his authority. Interest in that takes up 79.7 percent of the talk and deals
with "our administration" and "I the President" and "our party,
liberties, values."

He pays much less interest to factual social problems, only 10.6
percent, and 9.7 percent are finally paid to the disastrous nuclear
war and federal spending. Even together, this 20.3 percent social
interest is no match for the interest in his administration and in
his role as president. His 79.7 percent is an overwhelming interest in his political ego and power, but Reagan is not the only
one who showed this artful attitude. Lyndon Johnson was just
as concerned with his political ego when he discussed the Atlantic Alliance (K. Dovring, 1975). One of the advantages of a
democratic society is that free speech is a community value so
that any political communicator can choose whatever pattern of
communication he feels best serves his program and personality—totalitarian or democratic in diversity and compromise. But
people are also free to accept or reject his communications and
make up their own minds.[1]

Reagan could count upon both domestic and global publics
whether he wanted it or not when he made a speech. Many other
politicians have to fight for a place in the chorus of voices to get
attention. Among them is Moammar Qadhafi, ruler of the small
oilrich nation of Libya. In analysis of international communications we often talk about communicator-at-home *versus* communicator-abroad. As previously noted, this is not a geographic
description; it is the profile of a speaker, a classification of his
ideology. For instance, when a Chinese communist talks to his
fellow countrymen who embrace his doctrine, he is a communicator-at-home. But he is also "at home" when he talks to other
people around the globe, even if they don't speak Chinese, because they embrace the same political faith as he. There the
English lingua franca comes in handy. Then there is the communicator-abroad that the communist speaker, of course, be-

comes when he talks to dissenters in his own nation and everywhere else. On Main Street in a small American town we meet another communicator-abroad. He speaks American English—it is his mother tongue. He is a skinhead who is at home only when he speaks to other skinheads in the United States and in other nations. But he is very much abroad when he talks to other Americans who don't share his lifestyle.

In 1976, Qadhafi's *The Green Book* was published in London in two volumes. The first is in both Arabic and English, the second in English only. According to the publisher, "the book is aimed at the whole world." This is confirmed by the book's contents. It is Qadhafi's program for world revolution, which Qadhafi, the ruler of Libya, still does his level best to carry out at home and around the world. Recently he has offered a billion dollar gift to improve minorities' life in the United States. What is the philosophy behind such a gift? Is the humanitarian aspect on the offer its only character? According to the media, Qadhafi has lost his "good standing" in the world community and is looked upon as a "pariah." The offer was rejected by the American government.

The Green Book uses English as lingua franca to reach its worldwide public. His uses of ordinary English words are conspicuous. His book is in fact a kind of dictionary for the use of familiar, often political words in a new meaning. This is the world according to Qadhafi.

To get his general attitude we apply the same categories of analysis as we did on Reagan. What does Qadhafi identify with? What does he demand? What are his problems? From the book we get an overwhelming picture of a political figure who has very little power. His identifications cover only 23.2 percent of his message, and the demands are 28.4 percent. But his problems make up for this by their 48.4 percent presence. This is a politician who has no power to speak of, at least when he wrote his book. This is still true, globally speaking. In Libya today it is another matter.

In general, the book is a very negative document; the problems are always overwhelming, often between 80 percent and 90 percent of his messages in the different chapters of the book. There is no good side to record among them. The demands are few. Only in the sixth chapter, when he calls for revolution, do the demands dominate the message by 51.3 percent. In fact, there the demands turn out to be his real identifications. But one can also find a rare similarity in his approach when he talks about the press and its freedom. There the demands also dominate his message by 51.1 percent. We shall see later what kind of press freedom he demands.

The first volume of *The Green Book* advertises that it concerns "The Solution of the Problem of Democracy." Its subtitle is "The Authority of the People." The heart of the volume is the sixth chapter, "Popular Congresses and People's Committees." It also displays a map of how the whole society should be organized. The chapters are eight in all. The second volume is wholly devoted to the "Solution of the Economic Problems." Most demands in its various chapters dominate the identifications and problems. The situation is obviously tense at this time. Figures for demands and problems such as 67.9 percent, 78.4 percent, or 87.4 percent overwhelm his identification symbols amounting only to 32.1 percent, 21.6 percent, and 12.6 percent—not a strong sponsor for a reform. And when it comes to problems in his book, they are filled with agonizing thoughts about the troubles the reformer faces in a world described as hostile and miserable and filled with injustice against the people.

His book is also filled with familiar concepts from Western democracies and, as we said, is an illustration of the use of English as lingua franca. Important Western concepts such as democracy and a free press, Parliament and party are among those terms worth a closer look when he uses them. "Democracy" is for Qadhafi that "authority will be taken over by the masses." "Supervision of the people by the people, *not* supervision of the government by the people." It means "people's authority," "sovereignty of the people," which means "direct democracy" or "popular democracy" carried out by the "people as a whole." How can this happen? It happens when the "people are their own supervisors" since "democracy is the responsibility of the whole society." "This is the era of the masses and of poor people" and "democracy is the whole people" since "authority anchored in all the people is genuine democracy," and the "only true authority is in the people and the masses," which eventually will become "direct democracy in an orderly form." He then goes on in rich detail about how this "orderly form" is created. The base for everything is the masses of people who exercise supervision of themselves by creating congresses and committees, administrative people's committees, and other popular groups representing different professions and interests and working committees, all winding up together in "the popular congress" where all citizens are members and can watch out for each other and watch each other. The mass will supervise the execution of all this. This is the organization of "real democracy," and it will also "put an end to all forms of dictatorial rule in the world today." It should also be observed here that "minorities" among the mass are only looked upon as a part of the mass of people with no voice before they joined the people's mass movement. No special treatment is given since they are only a part of the whole. We shall come back to this later when we try to understand what philosophy is behind Qadhafi's billion dollar offer to "minorities" in the United States.

Eventually all the committees and congresses will come together in the "General People's Congress," which in its turn is supervised by all the people. In short, for anyone who still hasn't gotten the message: "democratic systems are a cohesive structure whose foundations are figuratively laid on basic popular congresses, people's committees and professional associates, all these come together in the General People's Congress," which is supervised by the people as a mass who also run all public utilities and see to it that "medical journals should only express medical facts, not policy."

In these few examples of what democracy is according to Qadhafi, there emerges a jargon concentrated on the people and the mass. These are undercurrents of meaning that the rest of the world has to cope with in a discussion about democracy with Qadhafi, but this is not the end of undercurrents in the concept of democracy. There are negative undercurrents of meanings that also give color to the general concept of democracy. There we get to know how Qadhafi looks at the rest of the world. Democracy is *not*: "excluding masses from power," "represent only a minority," "prevailing traditional democracy," "not acting on the people's behalf," "people are victims, are fooled, exploited, plundered of their sovereignty," exposed to "fraud," "one party system, two party system, multi party system," "sham democracy," "representation is fraud," "dividing people into constituents," "dictatorship established under false democracy is the reality of the political systems in the world today," "conflicts of classes and sects," "assumption of peoples authority," "representation is fraud," or "all isolation of the people from political activity."

All these concepts are repeated again and again, sometimes literally, sometimes with small variations. In any global conversation Qadhafi can appeal to "democracy" and use any of his undercurrents of meaning for the general concept. It is up to his opponents or followers to observe what he means. Consequences for the contacts can have both social and political repercussions.

His excuse for an aggressive policy is clear in his negative references to the rest of the globe. There, the "real trouble in the world are the existing governments, all over the world" and "all political systems in the world." "Conflict between classes" also contributes to this. There are no positive concepts here that Qadhafi can identify with.

Using the concept of "party," it is defined as "all the people," and "the whole people," which is the "society as a whole." What the party is *not* comes out in "contemporary dictatorship" that "makes a monkey of the people." "It is a deceitful farce," people are "bought and bribed." But this misery is no wonder because "political theories dominate the world today" and "people are victims of the party's struggle for power." We live in the "most oppressive tyrannical dictatorial age." The situation does not improve by all these opinion polls that "allowed (people) only to say yes or no" because "those who say yes, those who say no don't express their will."

Another Western key symbol is "Parliament." In Qadhafi's parlance it is, like "class," an absolutely negative concept. "Parliament government [*sic*] a means of plundering the people," "parliament [*sic*] most tyrannical dictatorship" where the "masses are completely isolated from their representatives." Parliament is also "a misleading solution."

The alternative to this is "participation by the people, not through activity of their representatives," and "popular Congresses—direct democracy ideal" with the "masses and all citizens members of the popular congress." This is the era of the masses who rise in "revolution" and "put an end to all forms of dictatorial rule in the world today." Now is the "end of the journey of the masses' movement in its quest for democracy." "Poor people, all the people, the whole people" participate in this "Popular Revolution."

Qadhafi is very clear when he considers the role of the press today. "Problem of press freedom cannot be solved unless the entire crises of democracy in the whole society can be solved." Just as in *The Green Book*'s volume on economics, the problem here is between private ownership and the masses. In economics it takes the expression of workers who labor for wages—a negative concept—and private owners—also a negative concept. There the state, that is the people, will take on all ownership in partnership with the workers, also the people. From this partnership there will come the "solution of the economic problem" with all the benefits described in detail.

The press problem also turns out to be a question of its ownership *versus* the public. According to Qadhafi, "the press is a means of expression of the society in the era of the masses," this "new era of the masses" that gives the "authority to the people" because "the press freedom is a problem of democracy." "The democratic press is that which is issued by a popular committee compounding all the various categories of society." This popular committee is, like the rest of "basic popular congresses" and "people's committees," all finally included in the "General People's Congress," which is supervised by the mass of the people while being made up by the people's different categories of professions and interests. The main thing is that the whole population is there to exercise its rights.

Then Qadhafi tells us what the press *cannot* be: "The press cannot be owned by either of those natural or corporate persons." "The press is not a means of expression of a natural or corporate person." Then he explains: "A natural person is an individual who has the right to speak only for himself." "He has the freedom to self expression even if . . . he behaves irrationally to express his madness," "The corporate person represents corporative interests and is free to express his corporate identity but represents no more than the group." Then, "any newspaper owned by an individual expresses only his viewpoint, not public opinion." The same goes for "trade journals or journal by the Chamber of Commerce who presents only its own point of view."

In fact, his thoughts on press freedom are the same as his undercurrents in all the Western concepts he has given us a glimpse of here; present interpretation of the concepts leads to the world's political disaster. Only the undercurrents of meaning and policy he gives the concepts can save the world. "Democracy" is the key symbol but according to Qadhafi's terms.

His language is the language of lingua franca. From his political philosophy it is clear that no individual or groups, such as minorities for instance, can act on its own. Only as part of the mass of the people can they exercise their rights. This means that when Qadhafi offers a "humanitarian gift" to another nation's minorities he does not mean that the gift does not carry some responsibilities. The gift is supposed to make the minorities a part of the whole mass of people who eventually must take over the government of a country if the minorities, together with the rest of the people, will be able to execute their political and social right. The gift is a way to give "people's revolution" a chance to succeed in agreement with Qadhafi's design for world revolution "in the era of the masses." Meanwhile, he is creating a jargon or vocabulary that, if permitted to emerge from the undercurrents, will create a political jargon close to the lingo of extreme movements of the past.

When the global world uses common community symbols, such as democracy, to get into contact, the lingua franca carries with it often some shades of different extreme meaning of political extremist vocabularies. But the global conversation is also made more difficult by the partisan twist any political party in the Western world makes in the use of their community symbols that now are used worldwide. Reagan's partisan communications were one example.

Then there are those who wholeheartedly swallow the literal expression of a symbol such as "democracy" and get confused in the process when they try to understand what a speaker means, be he at home or abroad. This fuzzy thinking is typical for many among us and has been going on from the beginning of time. It is only recently that engineers discovered the phenomenon worth research and even view the research as a "new science of fuzzy logic" (Kosko, 1993). Political speakers have always lived comfortably with fuzzy logic and thinking and will probably continue to do so. Meantime, one can wonder with Alice in Wonderland "whether you *can* make words mean so many different things." And Humpty Dumpty's answer said it all: "When I use a word . . . it means just what I choose it to mean—Neither more nor less. . . . The question is . . . which is to be master—that's all." Qadhafi is likely to agree.

NOTE

1. As we said, the communicator always starts out appealing to well-known community symbols. He changes them by replacing them partly or completely by words that, through context, point partly to the original community values. When this new meaning has been repeated many times—and there his gift as an artist is used—the community symbol receives a new undercurrent of meaning that eventually will replace the old community value. If the new meaning is repeated often enough it becomes commonplace, and a special vocabulary or jargon emerges. If it does not go that far, its undercurrent is often hidden and the public is exposed to "a new wine in old bottles." So it happens that "human rights" turn into "freedom of trade."

The analyst has to record both the literal appearance of the well-known community symbols and when and how often replacement in meaning then occurs. He also must record whether it eventually changes the original community value or if the change very soon disappears or only exists as a trace or sign of future developments. However, every such occurrence shall be recorded, or stored on files or in a computer so other analysts can check what has happened or is happening. But it is important to remember that the analysts deal with a creative artist when they study a political communicator, and that symbols and meanings are up for change any time the communicator wants to change the context in which the original values appear. The influence of this process is then analyzed by public opinion watchers. Often through history this change of meanings has created much speculation and confusion until it was made clear that it is the context of a concept that makes its meaning every time, and as soon the context changes, any concept follows suit.

References

Allende, Salvador. 1972. *No more dependence. Appeal to the world's conscience at the General Assembly of the United Nations on December 4, 1972.* Nottingham, Eng.: Bertrand Russell Peace Foundation.

Anderson, Martin. 1988. *Revolution.* San Diego, New York, and London: Harcourt, Brace Jovanovich.

Baron, Dennis. 1989. *Declining grammar and other essays on the English vocabulary.* Urbana, IL: National Council of Teachers of English.

————. 1990. *The English only question. An official language.* New Haven and London: Yale University Press.

Bartlett, Irving H. 1978. *Daniel Webster.* New York and London: W. W. Norton.

Bateson, Gregory. [1972] 1988. *Steps to an ecology of mind.* Northvale, NJ: Aronson.

————. 1988. *Mind and nature.* New York: Bantam.

Berelson, Bernard. 1952. *Content analysis in communication research.* Glencoe, IL: The Free Press.

Bolton, W. F. 1984. *The language of 1984: Orwell's English and ours.* Knoxville: The University of Tennessee Press.

Bush, George. 1988. Acceptance Speech, Republican National Convention, New Orleans. *New York Times,* August 19.

Carroll, Lewis (C.L. Dodgson). [1865, 1871] N.d. *Alice's adventures in Wonderland. Through the looking-glass. The hunting of the Snark.* New York: Random House.

Castro, Fidel. 1962. *Declarations of Havana*. Beijing: Foreign Languages Press.

Chervenkov, Vulko. 1950. *Tasks of the cooperative farms. Report delivered on April 5, 1950*. Sofia: Communist Party of Bulgaria.

China Today Magazine (American Edition). 1996. (October 10).

Clancy, Paul R. 1974. *Just a country lawyer. A biography of Senator Sam Erwin*. Bloomington and London: Indiana University Press.

Cooper, James Fenimore. [1826] 1960. *The last of the Mohicans*. New York: Washington Square Press.

Cronin, Vincent. 1978. *Catharine Empress of all the Russians*. New York: William Morrow.

de Tocqueville, Alexis. [1835] 1945. *Democracy in America*. New York: Alfred Knopf.

Dionne, E. J., Jr. 1991. *Why Americans hate politics*. New York: Simon & Schuster.

Djordjevic, Tome. 1988. *Komunikacija i vlas* (Communication and power). Beograd: Mladost. (Reviewed in *Socialist Thought and Practice*. 5–6 (May–June 1988): 108–10.)

Doder, Dusko, and Louise Branson. 1990. *Gorbachev. Heretic in the Kremlin*. New York: Viking Penguin.

Dovring, Folke. 1996. *Leninism: Political Economy as Pseudoscience*. Westport, CT: Praeger Publishers.

Dovring, Karin. 1951. *Striden kring sions sånger och närstående sångsamlingar*. Vols. 1–2. Lund: Gleerupska Universitetsbokhandeln.

———. 1959. *Road of propaganda. The semantics of biased communication*. Introduction by Harold D. Lasswell. New York: Philosophical Library.

———. 1965a. "Troubles with mass communication and semantic differentials in 1744 and today." *The American Behavioral Scientist* 9:1 (January): 9–14.

———. 1965b. "Land reform as a propaganda theme." In F. Dovring, *Land and Labor in Europe*, 3d rev. ed. The Hague: Martinus Nijhoff.

———. 1967. "Mass communication of news in a world of competition." *IPI Report, Monthly Bulletin of the International Press Institute* (Zurich, Switzerland). September, 7–8.

———. 1975. *Frontiers of communication. The Americas in search of political culture*. Boston: Christopher.

———. 1987. *Harold Dwight Lasswell: His communication with a future*. Urbana, IL: Author.

Febvre, Lucien. 1947. *Le problème de l'incroyance au xvie siècle. La religion de Rabelais*. Paris: Editions Albin Michel.

Gorbachev, Mikhail S. 1986. *A time for peace*. New York: Richardson & Steirman.

Gross, Bertram. 1980. *Friendly fascism. The new face of power in America*. New York: McEvans.

Gurevich, David. 1991. *From Lenin to Lennon: A memoir of Russia in the sixties*. San Diego, London, and New York: Harcourt Brace Jovanovich.

Hitler, Adolf. [1925–27] 1934. *Mein Kampf*. Vols. 1–2. München: Franz Eher.

Johnson, Haynes. 1991. *Sleepwalking through history. America through the Reagan years*. New York and London: W. W. Norton.

Key, Wilson Bryan. 1989. *The age of manipulation*. New York: Henry Holt.

Khrushchev, Nikita S. 1961. *Khrushchev's "Mein Kampf."* With background by Harrison E. Salisbury. (Contains new Soviet Communist Party Program.) New York: Belmont Books.

King, Dennis. 1989. *Lyndon LaRouche and the new American fascism*. New York: Doubleday.

King, Martin Luther, Jr. 1963. *Letter from Birmingham city jail*. Philadelphia: American Friends Service Committee.

Kosko, Bart. 1993. *Fuzzy thinking: The new science of fuzzy logic*. New York: Hyperion.

Kozol, Jonathan. 1985. *Illiterate America*. New York: Anchor Press/Doubleday.

Krippner, Stanley. 1980. *Human possibilities in mind exploration in the USSR and Eastern Europe*. Garden City, NY: Anchor Press, Doubleday.

Kurth, Peter. 1990. *American Cassandra: The life of Dorothy Thompson*. Boston, Toronto, and London: Little, Brown.

Lasswell, Harold D. 1927. *Propaganda technique in the world war*. London: Kegan Paul.

———. 1930. *Psychopathology and politics*. Chicago: University of Chicago Press.

———. 1951. *The world revolution of our time*. (Hoover Institute Studies.) Stanford, CA: Stanford University Press.

Lasswell, Harold D., and Dorothy Blumenstock. 1939. *World revolutionary propaganda. A Chicago study*. New York and London: Knopf.

Lasswell, Harold D., and Abraham Kaplan. 1950. *Power and Society. A framework for political inquiry*. New Haven, CT: Yale University Press.

Lasswell, Harold D., Nathan Leites, and Associates. 1949. *Language of politics. Studies in quantitative semantics*. New York: George W. Stewart.

Lasswell, Harold D., Daniel Lerner, and Ithiel de Sola Pool. 1952. *The comparative study of symbols.* (Hoover Institute Studies.) Stanford, CA: Stanford University Press.

Lisagor, Peter. 1961. "Do Russ. mean what they say? Glossary of Soviet jargon." *Chicago Daily News,* July 12.

Locke, John. [1690] 1979. *An essay concerning human understanding.* Edited by Peter Nidditch. Oxford: Oxford University Press.

Lutz, W. 1990. *Double speak.* New York: Harper and Collins.

Mao-tse-tung. 1967. *Quotations from Chairman Mao-tse-tung.* Introduction by A. Doak Barnett. New York: Bantam Books.

Martin, Judith. 1989. *Miss Manners' guide for the turn-of-the millennium.* New York: Pharos Books.

Mattera, Philip. 1990. *Prosperity lost.* Reading, MA and New York: Addison-Wesley.

McCrum, Robert, William Cowan, and Robert MacNeil. 1986. *The story of English.* New York: Penguin.

Melville, Herman. 1851. *Moby Dick, or the white whale.* New York: Harper and Brothers.

Miller, John C. 1936. *Sam Adams, pioneer in propaganda.* Stanford, CA: Stanford University Press

Mitford, Nancy. 1953. *Madame de Pompadour. A biography.* New York: Random House.

Morris, Desmond. 1994. *Bodytalk.* New York: Crown Publishers.

Moynihan, Daniel Patrick. 1978. "Distortion of political language." *Washington Post,* November 21, A19.

Muth, Rodney, and Mary M. Finley, and Marcia F. Muth. 1990. *Harold D. Lasswell. An annotated bibliography.* New Haven, CT and Dordrecht: New Haven Press and Kluwer Academic Publishers.

Noonan, Peggy. 1990. *What I saw at the revolution: A political life in the Reagan era.* New York: Random House.

Nydell, Margaret K. 1987. *Understanding Arabs: A guide for westerners.* Yarmouth, ME: Intercultural Press.

Orlov, Yuri. 1991. *Dangerous thoughts. Memoirs of a Russian life.* Translated from Russian by Thomas P. Whitney. New York: William Morrow.

Orwell, George (Eric Blair). [1949] 1958. *Nineteen eighty-four. A novel.* Harmondsworth, Middlesex (England): Penguin Books.

Peron, Eva. 1952. *La razón de mi vida.* Buenos Aires: Ediciones Peuser.

Peterson, Theodore B. 1964. *Magazines in the twentieth century.* 2d ed. Urbana: University of Illinois Press.

Pool, Ithiel de Sola, et al. 1951. *Symbols of internationalism.* (Hoover Institute Studies.) Stanford, CA: Stanford University Press.

———. 1952. *Symbols of democracy.* (Hoover Institute Studies.) Stanford, CA: Stanford University Press.

Porter, Rosalie Pedaline. 1991. *Forked tongue: The politics of bilingual education.* New York: Basic Books.

Powers, Ron. 1977. *The newscasters.* New York: St. Martin's Press.

Pozner, Vladimir. 1990. *Parting with illusions.* New York: The Atlantic Monthly Press.

Prospect for America. The Rockefeller panel report. 1961. Garden City, NY: Doubleday.

Qadhafi, Muammar. 1976. *The green book.* London: Martin Bryan and O'Keeffe.

The Quarterly Review of Doublespeak. Urbana, IL: National Council of Teachers of English.

Regan, Donald T. 1988. *For the record: From Wall Street to Washington.* San Diego, CA, New York, and London: Harcourt Brace Jovanovich.

Rheingold, Howard. 1988. *They have a word for it: A light-hearted lexicon of untranslatable words and phrases.* New York: Jeremy P. Tarcher.

Safire, William. 1991. *Coming to terms.* New York: Doubleday.

Schiefer, Bob and Gary Paul Gates. 1989. *The acting president.* New York: E. F. Dutton.

Sheehy, Gail. 1990. *The man who changed the world. The lives of Mikhail Gorbachev.* New York: Harper Collins.

Smith, Hedrick. 1990. *The new Russians.* New York: Random House.

Sokolov, Raymond. 1985. "Changing tunes at the French culture ministry." *Wall Street Journal,* January 17.

Solzhenitsyn, Alexandr. 1978. "The West has lost its courage." *Washington Post,* June 11 (Sunday), C1.

Sorokin, Vladimir. 1985. *The Queue.* Translated with an introduction by Sally Laird. New York: Readers International.

Stevenson, Robert Louis. [1883] 1966. *From Scotland to Silverado . . .* Edited by James D. Hart. Cambridge, MA: Belknap Press of Harvard University Press.

Sturluson, Snorri. [A.D. 1179–1241] 1950. *Edda.* Edited by Anne Holtsmark and Joh Helgason, 2d ed. København, Oslo, and Stockholm: Ejnar Munksgaard, Dreyers Forlag and Svenska Bokförlaget/ Norstedt.

Tanguy-Prigent (Pierre François). 1950. *Démocratie à la terre.* Paris: Editions de la Liberté.

Tegner, Esaias, Jr. [1870, 1874] 1922–25. *Ur Språkens värld.* Vols. 1–2. Stockholm: Bonniers Förlag. (Includes, i.a., *Språkets makt över tanken,* 1870 and *Språk och Nationalitet,* 1874).

Twain, Mark (S. L. Clemens). [1869] 1966. *The innocents abroad, or the new pilgrims progress.* New York, Scarborough, Ont., and London: New American Library and The New English Library.

————. [1884] 1953. *The adventures of Huckleberry Finn.* (In *Tom Sawyer and Huckleberry Finn.*) London and Glasgow: Collins.

————. [1893–94] 1970. *Pudd'nhead Wilson.* Toronto, New York, and London: Bantam Books.

Ustinov, Peter. [1990] 1991. *The old man and Mr. Smith. A fable.* New York: Arcade Publishing, Little, Brown.

Vygotsky, L. S. [1934, 1956] 1962. *Thought and language.* Edited and translated by Eugenia Hanfmann and Gertrude Vakar. Boston, MA, New York, and London: The MIT Press and John Wiley.

Whorf, Benjamin Lee. 1956. *Language, thought and reality.* New York: Wiley.

Wiesel, Elie. 1988. Interview. *TV Guide,* December 31.

Winterowd, W. Ross. 1989. *The culture and politics of literacy.* New York and Oxford: Oxford University Press.

Wright, Karen. 1990. "The road to the global village." *Scientific American* 262 (March): 83–85.

Yeltsin, Boris. 1990. *Against the grain.* New York and London: Summit Books.

Yule, Sir Henry and Arthur Coke Burnell. 1886. *Hobson-Jobson, being a glossary of Anglo-Indian colloquial words and phrases.* London: John Murray.

Index

About the Author

KARIN DOVRING is a communications analyst. Born and raised in Sweden, she worked as a journalist in Europe and was for many years an associate of Harold Lasswell of Yale Law School. She has published several books, including *Road of Propaganda*. She is also a poet with three published collections and was recently elected into the *International Poetry Hall of Fame* by the National Library of Poetry.

ISBN 0-275-95878-7

90000>

EAN

9 780275 958787

HARDCOVER BAR CODE